TIOMNAIM AN IARRACHT SO DO M' CHÉILE MONICA,
DO M' CHLANN MHAC,
DO CARMEL, MAURA, AGUS FÍÓNA BEAG,
AGUS GO MÓRMÓR DO MHUINTIR CHLÉIRE.

THE MERCIER PRESS LTD.
4 Bridge Street, Cork; 25 Lower Abbey Street, Dublin 1.

© Riobárd P. Breatnach, 1975

ISBN 0 85342 433 0

The Man from Cape Clear

A TRANSLATION

by

RIOBÁRD P. BREATNACH

of

Conchúr Ó Síocháin's *Seanchas Chléire*

THE MERCIER PRESS
DUBLIN and CORK

'Ceo, Ceol agus Seoltóireacht—Trí Pairteanna den Draíocht.'
'Fog, Music and Sailing—Three Portions of Magic.'

A Cape Clear Proverb

ACKNOWLEDGEMENTS

Tá mé fé chomaoin mhóir ag Rev. Dr. Pádraig Ó Fiannachta, Professor of Medieval and Early Modern Irish, *Coláiste Phádraig, Má Nuad,* for his painstaking attention and prompt replies to lengthy queries on a wide range of matter relating to the original Irish work. Any short-comings in the use I made of his generous scholarship are solely my responsibility.

It is a privilege to pay tribute to the forbearance of Pádraig Ó Maidín, the Cork County Librarian, who was so unstinted in sharing with me his far-ranging knowledge of source material on Cork and on all things Irish.

My sincere thanks are also due to the following for assistance in the course of the book's progress : Prof. R. A. Breatnach, Head of the Irish Department and the members of *Roinn na Gaeilge* at University College, Cork; Dr. E. Fahy, Lecturer in Geography at the University, and his Department's Cartographer, Seán Riordan; Máire Ní Choileáin, B.A., of the University's Typing Pool; Nóra Browne, M.A., Assistant Librarian, and the Staff of the University's Main Library.

All my fellow-islanders on *Inis Arcáin* (Sherkin Island) have borne with patience my persistent probing of their rich fund of knowledge about the old days, especially Willie Norris and Michael MacCarthy.

Last but not least, I thank Caoimhín Ó Marcaigh, a Director of the Mercier Press, for his guidance and patience. Buíochas óm' chroí dhó!

The map in this book is based on the Ordnance Survey by permission of the Government (Permit No. 2351).

FOREWORD

Medium and Mode

Jorge Luis Borges is a cult-figure in the current literary world. In a well-known essay 'The Argentine Writer and Tradition' he has asserted that 'the idea that a literature must define itself in terms of its national traits is a relatively new concept', and that the belief that 'writers must seek themes from their own countries' is equally new and arbitrary. He opposes these views with the thesis that 'our patrimony is the universe', and claims that it was enough for men like Shaw, Berkeley and Swift 'to feel Irish' in order to be different, and so capable of being 'innovators in English culture'.[1] One can readily understand why a critic and writer such as Borges, born into the atmosphere of the flux of the colonial and expatriate cultures in the Argentine, would see fit to spurn national traits and themes and cultivate the cosmopolitan. The latin tag *quidquid recipitur recipitur ad modum recipientis* could not apply in such a young and ethnically mixed country as the Argentine for there was no distinctive *modus,* no mould, to receive the borrowings from the national cultures of the Western world. If the culture of the indigenous inhabitants had anything of its own to offer it was insufficient to induce the conquerors to put down roots, start anew, and sever their umbilical cords with their European origins. In any event it would be scorned as something wearing the stigma of the primitive—even if it came to be known. All this explains why Borges uses such specious arguments in support of his contention as those he bases on the fact that, for example, Shakespeare and Racine used many borrowed plots for their plays, stories that were not of native origin. But what are we to think of the implications of his second proposition about feeling Irish in order to be an innovator in English culture? Putting aside the bland assumption or paradox behind the statement, I do not think that it is an exercise in irascible obscurantist nationalism to ask how Irish one should feel in order to be an innovator in Irish culture.

It seems clear to me that Borges's special situation has made him blind to two facts that I deem to be axioms. Firstly, the linguistic medium of a literary work has well-nigh absolute

significance in determining its *raison d'être,* for a language and
a literature are of each other as are the dye and the cloth. To
think otherwise is to fail to see that, as Ernst Cassirer put it,
each language draws 'a magic circle' around the people who
use it. This circle encloses the cluster of immemorial connota-
tions that cling to every single word in any particular language
that has grown and been shaped in human hearts and minds as
the 'mountainous and anonymous work of unconscious generations' (*Language,* Edward Sapir, London, 1949, p. 220). In fine
those who speak different languages live in different 'worlds of
reality'. Secondly, the modes by which, or the moulds in which
a people shape their particular 'world of reality' will also differ.
This is an obvious corollary to the individuality of each language with all its semantic entailments; syntactic, aural, and
associative.[2]

These prefatory remarks may well appear to be pedantically
pretentious in relation to literary matter that has, for many, the
mark of primal, if not primitive simplicity. This is a mistaken
standpoint. In the first place one does not parody what is light-
weight or ephemeral in the literary sense—as Flann O'Brien
(Myles na gCopaleen) did in his *An Béal Bocht,* recently translated into English as *The Poor Mouth.* In the second—and this,
I think, bears out my point about parody—in comparison with
the autobiographies no other body of literary work resulting
from the revival of Irish has had such an influence on those who
know Irish, or such an impact on those who only know writing
in Irish through translations. And this holds especially for the
acknowledged masterpieces from the Great Blasket Island.
Lastly, I recall seeing in a French newspaper an article written
by a Member of the French Academy whose name I have
forgotten. This article is about a meeting with James Joyce, but
in the first paragraph the writer mentions his having recently
read a particular book which left such an impression on him
that he does not hesitate to compare its author with Gorki,
Pilnyak, and Chekhov. He notes that this writer can, however,
be distinguished from those by his being devoid of the note of
bitterness with his lot. The book in question was none other
than Maurice O'Sullivan's *Twenty Years A-Growing.* Significantly, the Academician added that as he read the work in its

English version he must have lost much and that he would have dearly loved to have been able to read the original.

In the light of the preceding there is, it seems to me, a stronger case to be made for the importance of some of these autobiographies than the one that is based solely on the unqualified and warm enthusiasm of E. M. Forster which may be summed up in some words of his Introductory Note to the English translation of *Fiche Blian ag Fás* (*Twenty Years A-Growing*) : 'This book is unique.' Even more important than the unequivocal character of this verdict of Forster's is his remark that while Synge and others described the life of the *Gaeltachts* 'from the outside', O'Sullivan did so 'from the inside'; and so once more I must insist that the linguistic vehicle is an integral and indivisible part of the whole process of the writing 'from the inside'. Being 'inside' in the merely physical sense is inadequate, allowing even that one is *au fait* with the language, to a lesser or greater degree, as Synge was. Again if the exercise of paraphrasing within the ambit of one language is a futility in that nobody's 'own words' could stand, as Aldous Huxley remarked for Shakespeare's, it is equally true that Synge's Hiberno-English, no matter how faithful it *was* to an actual spoken idiom, could only have an evanescent verisimilitude.

A brief word about the 'mode' or 'the mould' of the autobiographies. What more natural extension of the role of the *seanchaí* (or oral story-teller) could there be than his emergence in a literate age as the innovator of a native mode in which his art could find freer play and fresh life! And where was this development more likely to occur at its best than in 'the far south-west of Ireland (which) is in many ways a region apart, a region of cultural refuge'?[3] The conjunction of inherited craft and timely stimulus happened first on the Great Blasket where it became possible to mirror, without distortion, the real facts of Irish life, of the Hidden Ireland we might say, in the mother tongue for the very first time, and with an authenticity that touches the very quick of our identity.

The Genre
Despite all that had been achieved in Irish writing up to the

late twenties of this century, especially in what I might venture to call the pure Parnassian idiom of Peadar Ó Laoire, the book which told the story of Tomás Ó Criomhthain's life on the Great Blasket—*An t-Oileánach* (*The Islandman*), published in 1929— was a blinding revelation. Within seven years it was followed by two other autobiographies from the island : Muiris Ó Súileabháin's *Fiche Blian ag Fás* (*Twenty Years A-Growing*) published in 1933, and *Peig* (1936), the book in which Peig Sayers became the first woman to write in Irish the story of her life. These 'Blasket' books, each so individual in temper and style, have enriched us with their blessed gift of as full and rich a canvas of a tiny community's life as has ever been painted. Together they are a truly remarkable phenomenon, unmatched in the whole world of literature, and one made poignant by the fact that the island which nourished such genius is now dumb. In 1940, four years after Peig Sayers had closed the story of her life with the words *Tá an seana-shaol imithe* (the old times are finished), Conchúr Ó Síocháin's *Seanchas Chléire* (lit. *The Story of Cape Clear*) was published and, for the first time, a voice from another island spoke.

It is not my purpose here to assess the full significance and comparative merits of the whole corpus of autobiographies in Irish.[4] I am not qualified for the task. My sole aim is to venture —and not without considerable qualms about my competence— to make some general critical comments on the striking tryptych composed of the volumes by Ó Criomhthain, Ó Súileabháin and Ó Síocháin, before dealing more fully with the Cape Clear man's book about which I feel that I will be on firmer ground.

Although the three differ greatly in character and personality, and the last comes from a different island, they are all the spokesmen of what is essentially the same communal ethos, just as would be the painter of a tryptych who had worked on his panels at widely-separated intervals over a long life. O'Sullivan's *Twenty Years A-Growing* (1933) was the first of the three to appear in an English translation and, as I have already noted, it made a profound impression on the major English novelist and critic, E. M. Forster. It was for him a remarkable 'account of neolithic civilisation from the inside'. If he had been asked, and was willing to write a Prefatory Note to Ó Crohan's *The*

Islandman when the English version appeared in 1937, he would have had to use the term 'palaeolithic' or, at very least, 'mesolithic' to describe the quality of the book, for the dominant tone of Ó Crohan is, by comparison, far more sombre and his whole vision of life considerably starker and more 'primitive' than O'Sullivan's. It would have been wiser, and more fitting perhaps, to have shunned such archaeological terms, and to draw rather on the vocabulary of the History of Ideas to describe both works. In such a context Forster would probably say that while Ó Crohan described a life that exemplified 'hard primitivism', O'Sullivan's book, being that of a much younger man— for he was born in 1904, that is forty-eight years after Ó Crohan —is an example of 'soft primitivism'. One should be slow to use all such analogical terms, however, not simply because they do not, in general, help us a great deal in making an evaluation of the books, but because they smack of condescension, and are wildly misleading in view of the latest theories of anthropologists about the nature of primitivism. Neither Ó Crohan nor O'Sullivan are 'primitive' writers in any valid sense, nor have they written works which describe a primitive or neolithic culture. There is far more savagery and sadism and infinitely less refinement in the bulk of modern novels than is to be found in either and, unlike far too many moderns, they do not venture into purlieus of the human mind of which no manner of art can make anything more than sterile territory. Nevertheless they hold the mirror steadily up to life and 'deal boldly with substantial things'—with the elemental pieties of their community— Ó Crohan with a gravity of spirit that is fused with a willing acceptance of the inscrutable ways of Providence, O'Sullivan with an irrepressible gaiety of heart that is a celebration of the festal spirit of a life that is no whit the less *sub facie aeternitatis*. Both, however, are at one in the belief that their whole way of life is dying. The older has done his best 'to set down the character of the people about me so that some record of us might live after us for the like of us will never be again' (*meon na ndaoine a bhí im thimpeall a chur síos chun go mbeadh ár dtuairisc ár ndiaidh mar ná beidh ár leithéidí arís ann*—lch. 265); and, lest we mistake the full import of this extract from the last pages of his book, he adds : 'One day there will be none left in the Blasket of all I have mentioned in this book—and none to remember them', (*Beidh an Blasgoad lá gan éinne den dream atá luaite agam sa leabhar so—ná éinne go mbeidh cuimhne aige orainn*—lch. 265). The younger one when he returns to the Blasket on holidays sees that 'There was a great change there after two years : green grass growing on the paths because no one walked them; five or six houses closed and the people gone out to the mainland . . .' (*Ba mhór an t-atharú i gceann dhá bhliain é: féar glas ag fás ar na casáin 'cheal siubhlóide; cúig nó sé do thithe dúnta agus na daoine imithe amach ar an mín-tír . . .*—lch. 376). The foreboding of the young man had been the finality of conviction of the older when he wrote almost a decade before him. On the other hand, the man from Cape Clear never even dreams that such a fate could face his island.

SEANCHAS CHLÉIRE (The Man from Cape Clear)

The Cape Clear *Gaeltacht* (Irish-speaking district) still lives, and it is cheering to know that the affirmative confidence of the man who wrote its story, as he saw it, was not misplaced. The last panel in our tryptych looks to the future, not the past, for the light still shines as sure and certain as the Fastnet's beams, although the island is the sole survivor of the beleaguered Irish-speaking islands around the coast of the southern half of our country. The blessing that the author called down over thirty years ago, on the young generation of the island, who would not rest content with any particular bettering of their lot, has not gone unanswered. A new spirit is at work in the island, a groundswell that is heartening for all those who, whatever the odds, long for the revival of

> The speech that wakes the soul in withered faces,
> And wakes remembrance of great things gone by.[5]

It must always be kept in mind that even at present Cape Clear has a population that, despite the decline in numbers from the figure of over a 1,000 in pre-Famine days to slightly less than 200 today, is still bigger than that of the Great Blasket at any time in its history. Even more significant is the fact that Cape

Clear Island is the last surviving stronghold of the *Erainn* whose language and culture—though Celtic—were pre-Godelic, and who gave the Irish language a substratum of homely words borrowed by the *Gaeil* from the *Iarnbelre* or language of the *Erainn*—the dominant people in the south of the country before it was overrun by the *Goidel* (mod. *Gaeil*). The title *Corcu Loigde* (al. *Corca Laidhe*), which was the name of the sept whose chiefs were the O'Driscolls (<*Ó Drisceoil*, older *Ua Eidirsceoil*), 'the foremost representatives of the *Erainn*', still survives in the words 'Collymore' and 'Collybeg', the names of two districts bordering the River Ilen.[6]

If one needed one last proof of the immemorial antiquity of the historical roots which should make Cape Clear as exciting to the spirit as its jagged 'Viking-faced' cliffs are thrilling to the sight, we have but to recall the astonishing survival of such pre-Christian first names as Eireamháin and Maccon among the O'Driscolls of the island down to our own time.

Yet, by and large, it must be admitted that, until comparatively recent years, the Cape seems to have been the least familiar or frequented of the *Gaeltachtaí* since the beginning of the revival in 1893. Perhaps this accounts, to some extent, for the fact that only one voice has as yet spoken out on its behalf. The spur given to the latent potential of Ó Crohan's talents by such men as Brian O'Kelly, Carl Marstrander and Robin Flower was wanting in Cape Clear, it would seem, until Frs. Timothy Richardson and Donnchadh Ó Floinn became visitors to the island—some twenty years after Robin Flower's first sojourn on the Great Blasket in 1910. In the long run, however, all we can do is speculate for the bird of inspiration will settle where it lists.

When Ó Síocháin's book was published in 1940 readers of Irish were introduced to a community that in spite of the basic homogeneity of the large nineteenth century Irish-speaking population, differed significantly from that of the Great Blasket. Ó Síocháin himself is his own man. Wisely, or unwisely, his cicerones do not seem to have read Gorki or Loti to him as did Brian O'Kelly to Ó Crohan. Yet Ó Síocháin subtly stamps his unobtrusive personality on a narrative that rather records objectively, if still memorably, the many-sided life of the islanders than it reflects the reactions of the author in the 'intimate' way that Ó Crohan reveals his own 'natural critical faculty' (Robin Flower), and his gifts of irony and of what speakers of Irish call *stuaim* (steadiness, moderation, balance, control, etc.). The man from the Cape gives the reins more fully to the onward thrust of his narrative because his material world is more varied and spacious than the circumscribed one of Ó Crohan, more manifestly in the mainstream of history. There is a delightful incident described towards the end of Ó Síocháin's ninth chapter which tells how Fr. Labhrás Ó Mathúna, the early nineteenth century priest-poet of the island, dipped the multi-coloured, richly decorated habit of the author's great grand-mother in a pot of boiling bark, as he thought that one colour was more in keeping with the clay of the grave (*. . . ní oireann aon órnáid don chré*). I think that this is a fairly just image of the difference between Ó Síocháin's book and Ó Crohan's. A lyrical and descriptive colouring is threaded through the weft and woof of *Twenty Years A-Growing* which makes it *sui generis;* its horizon, too, is more extensive than that of *The Islandman.*

Again if there is no 'king', no neighbouring *cailleach* (Flower's 'gray-haired hag'), no Sunshine Diarmuid or Bald Tom in the story of Cape Clear, neither are there in the Blasket volumes such chapters as those of Ó Síocháin (Chapters 7 and 8) which present us with the embryonic novel that might have developed in Irish, one that would reveal the obverse side of the coin of colonial power as epitomised in the Big House and the Royal Writ. But comparisons are odious. I merely wish to make it clear that *Seanchas Chléire* complements rather than over-laps the massive achievement of the writers of the tiny Blasket community.

I have already mentioned the more capacious milieu open to Ó Síocháin, in the physical as well as the historical sense. This may be briefly illustrated by a resumé of the contents of his first chapter. While it opens with the accustomed glimpses of family background and island life we are speedily made aware of the importance of the place as a telegraphic base for transatlantic steamers down to 1866, the very year in which the author was born. The historical matter which follows includes a brief account of an episode during O'Donovan Rossa's visit to Cape (the common name for the island on the English-speaking mainland), and the islanders' ancestral memory of the tragic story of the death of Morty Oge O'Sullivan in 1754, which ends with the Lament composed by his attendant, Dónal Ó Conaill, on the eve of his execution in Cork. Such material, taken with the valuable and vivid details about a host of occupations, especially fishing, is rich compensation for any lack of the splendid character profiles and lively narrative passages in the Blasket books. And that is far from being all that could be said here, as the reader will quickly discover for himself.

Before I end this introduction I must take up again my earlier reference to the affirmative message of Ó Síocháin's book. Never for a moment does he envisage the island's being abandoned, and when he describes the past his purpose is not its preservation—as if in a memorial reliquary—merely for the contemplation of coming generations. He rather makes the past accessible in the full confidence *go n-adófaí an tine arís agus go dtosnódh sí ar adhaintiú i ndiaidh ar ndiaidh go mbeadh sí ina lán fuinnimh comh lasmhar agus a bhí sí cheana,* ('that the fire would be kindled again so as to flame up gradually until it would be fully a-blaze, and as glowing and radiant as it was before'—Chapter 17). And here the writer is thinking of the inner fire of the Irish language in whose phoenix flame the people's will would be annealed; for he knew that once such a fire begins to burn the smouldering turf will be handed on from generation to generation as it was from house to house in the olden days. Aspiring to what the present generation could have accomplished, but so shamefully failed to do, he bestowed his benediction on all who belonged to it: *Bheirimid a bhuíochas le Dia an tsoinseáil ar fheabhas a tháinig sa tsaol. Ach an dream óg atá ann anois, teastaíonn tuilleadh uathu ... Go mbua Dia leo, cé ná beadsa ann, ná scéala uaim* ('We thank God for the change for the better that has come about. But those who are young today want more ... May God prosper them—although I won't be there or tidings of me'—Chapter 14). I echo his words and say, in a phrase that occurs in his book: *Go dtagaidh a ghuth fén ngairm aige.* (May his prophecy be fulfilled.)

A NOTE ON THE TRANSLATION

'Translation from one language into another one ... is like looking at a Flemish tapestry with the wrong side out.'

—Cervantes

What I am about to write will fall far short of being an adequate treatment of the problems of translation at large, and even of the particular ones involved in translating Irish into English. To deal with the whole question satisfactorily one would need to write a lengthy essay, even a book.

Translation is an art but—old as it is—an art without a Muse. Perhaps Pandora might fit the part, since 'hope' lay at the bottom of her baneful box; and that is all the translator can do. Indeed he is not left with even that solace if he believes the well-known Italian tag: *Traduttore traditore.*

The problems posed by the rendering from one language into another of any matter that is not purely scientific are hydra-headed, and these are aggravated in translating from Irish into English, not only by a basic antinomy between the languages but by the existence of many forms of Hiberno-English, both artificial and actual. The fabricated forms of 'Kiltartanese' and its ilk are clearly unusable as they are only appropriate to the comic, freakish quaintness of the stage-Irish tradition. The actually existent are of necessity ephemeral since they are being constantly eroded by the irresistible levelling impact of a homogenised Anglo-American English. Moreover, as it is a truism that a translation ages more quickly than the original the obstacles facing a translator from Irish into English would appear to be well-nigh insurmountable.

Let the hazards be as numerous as they can be, translation is, as Goethe nevertheless insists, 'one of the most important, worthwhile concerns in the totality of human affairs'. To agree with him is not of course to desire the death of a single one of the world's 3,000 to 4,000 languages at the hands of the arrogant empires of a few major ones.

What to do then? I deliberately refrained from reading any of the translations of the other autobiographies in Irish through fear of being influenced by them, and set about my task with one aim in mind : to produce a version which while it would be readily intelligible to those ignorant of Irish would yet preserve something of the flavour of Irish as Provençal has preserved a *parfum du latinité*. I was somewhat encouraged to do so by what I read in a review of a translation from Italian in which the English critic considered the somewhat 'un-English' character of the language worthy of definite commendation.

In order to retain a little of the tang of the original Irish some 'stretching' of the English was called for; but this was balanced by the 'tightening' of syntactic and stylistic elements in the original which English-speaking readers would find tiresome or repetitive. As to my success or failure only the ordinary readers can be the final arbiters.

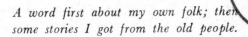

CHAPTER ONE

A word first about my own folk; then
some stories I got from the old people.

Youth has gone, alas, and old age has come; and when I look
back on all the years of my life melancholy fills my heart; still,
no one can be young for ever, and 'youth never comes a second
time.'

My father was heard to say that he was the eighth generation
in the place : so that tells that we are a long-established stock
on the Island.[1] The old house in which I was born is always
there, roof and all, although it is a hundred and three years
since it was built : 'the old stakes still remain but the hand that
arranged them lives no longer.' It was my grandfather built it
in his time, and his name was Conchúr also, like mine; however,
it wasn't there he himself was in the start of his days but in
another part of the Island. It was during his lifetime that the
landlords first alloted set portions of the land in shares; up to
that each one had only a garden-patch here, another there, and
a third elsewhere—with perhaps no two patches close together.
When it was divided-up my grandfather got a choice from the
landlord : to stay where he was or to shift to another place. He
chose to move, and he had his reason for doing so; none of the
family would stay in the old place in which he was. His wife—
that is my grandmother—said to him that a change was a good
thing 'even if you only moved from the hollow to the hill-side.'

Although the new dwelling wasn't big or roomy, it was a nice
little house—cosy, compact, sound, and in a healthy spot. It
was divided into two parts, a kind of kitchen and 'the room
below', the latter was the place where we slept, and it was
separated from the kitchen by a partition with a door in its
centre—giving entry to the bedroom. Outside the house itself
there were two 'rooms', the southern one and the northern. The
cows were kept in one of them, and the potatoes in the other
one.[2]

Three more children were born to them after they came to
live in the new house, two sons and a daughter who all survived.
Their names were Tomás, Peadar, and Máire. When they grew

1

and reached the age for marriage Tomás left and married into a house in the townland closest to him. A few years afterwards Máire followed suit and settled down in the same townland as Tomás. That left no one in the house but the old pair and Peadar, and later in the same year in which his sister left he married a woman named Cáit O'Driscoll; she was my mother.

They had eight children, six sons and two daughters, and I was the eldest of the family. When we grew up to become men and women there was a change coming in the world, with an odd one here and there building a new house and abandoning the old cabins. We said to one another that before we would scatter we would build a new house while we were still all together. At first my father was reluctant enough to give us permission to do so, and to leave the old place, but at last he was satisfied. That took place thirty-seven years ago.

The same *Gaeltacht* was there at that time as is there today : but, if so, the help to be got from the Government at that time was very little.

I used to hear many stories being told by my father about the things that happened during his own life. I heard him saying that he recalled when there was neither tea nor sugar there, and not even the matches that would light a fire or redden a pipe. The way they would kindle a fire, he said, was with some flint and steel, and a cotton rag, specially set aside for the purpose. When the flint was struck by the metal a spark would ignite the rag so that it would catch fire straightaway. No sooner was the rag ablaze than it would be put under a handful of straw that was ready in the fireplace; on top of the straw were placed fragments of partly-burned turf that were on the fireplace from the previous night, and there was the fire alight at once. As soon as your neighbours saw the smoke rising up from the chimney they came—one from here, one from there—seeking a 'spark' from the fire, that is to say anyone who hadn't the means in his own place to kindle one. Each messenger was given a piece of a burning turf-sod wrapped in a handful of straw.

Another thing he used to say was that neither coal nor paraffin was in use at that time; instead every four or five households went into partnership in order to buy a stack between them to bring in from the mainland. After unloading the turf they shared it, with the help of a basket, on the strand where the boat was beached, and everyone carried his own portion home. In order to do this particular job they waited until November for usually the wind blew then from the north-east and the sea was calm; it was fair weather that suited them for the boats were low in the water with the stacks high above the gunnels in them. They used bring in fuel for a half-year at that time : as the old man used to say, 'St Bridget's Feast Day —half the food left and half the fuel.'

With regard to providing light, since there was no paraffin there they had train-oil instead. They used to take the livers from hake or cod to that end, and put them all together in a big, capacious vat or in a spacious open tub. To cure them then for the special purpose they first shook a handful of salt over them; after that the container was left in the open air for the sun to draw the oil out of the livers. This was skimmed by using a large shell and was put in a jar or bottles which were well-corked. There was a special appliance for burning it—that is a *slige* or creuset. The oil was poured into it and whittled rushes were used as wicks. If the woman of the house wanted to go into any corner of the house she would dip a rush in the oil, light it and take it with her in her hand. That was the kind of light they had at that time, and it was a poor, dim thing indeed.[3]

About sixty-seven years ago there was a telegraph to Cape Clear from Baltimore through Sherkin Island. A submarine cable stretched across the sound from the western end of Sherkin, that is from Tracroo in Sherkin to Foilcoo, which is a strand in the eastern part of the Cape. There the first pole stood on the top of the strand and so they rose one after another, as is usual with their likes, until they reached the other end of the island that is the strand of South Harbour where the tele-graph office had been built for the business. The reason it was set up there was in order that news and messages could be taken there from the steamers on their way to England from America; for the entrance to South Harbour was the place appointed for every ship appearing on the coast to send their messages ashore.

There were three clerks in the office, and they had a look-out man on Slieve Ard, the high hill west of the harbour. The latter was ever and always watching for the first sight of a steamer, both day and night. If one were to come from the west at night he had a lantern by which he used send signals to the crew of the boat waiting on the strand; they were there for one sole purpose, that is to await an order from the look-out man. At the same time a messenger was sent straightaway to summon one of the clerks. The boat was launched and off it went. As soon as the steamer hove to the clerk shouted at the top of his voice asking the vessel's name, and the captain answered him. It was the clerk's turn to speak again and this is what he used to say: *Heave out all despatches on board, Reuters' newspapers, parcels for Queenstown and Cape Clear telegraph.* That is how I used hear one of the men from the boat's crew saying it as he mimicked the manner in which the clerk spoke. The despatches and the rest were packed in waterproof canisters so that there was no fear of the papers getting wet. The tin cans were lifted into the boat which returned to the strand; they were then brought to the office and opened by the clerk there; he used then send off the messages so that they would reach a merchant over in England three hours sooner than if they had been left aboard the ship until it reached the Cove of Cork.[4]

At the very same time that the telegraph was in Cape Clear there was a six-oared mail-boat travelling between the Cape and Baltimore; these two things, the telegraph and the mail-boat, were connected with one another and under the one authority. I heard my father saying that he was one of the crew of the mail-boat at that time; and just as occurs this very day passengers used to travel out to the mainland and into the Island according as their activities and businesses demanded. It was just at that time that O'Donovan Rossa, the Fenian Captain, lived in Skibbereen—something it is scarcely necessary for me to tell as everyone has heard of him.[5] However, since I'm drawing down the story, he paid a visit to the Cape by the mail-boat one day. There's a rock in the middle of the passage between Cape Clear and Sherkin, and its name is Gaiscanaun. Over this rock rushes the fiercest tidal currents anywhere on the coast. When the boat on its way into the Island drew close to the rock

4

one of the men said to O'Donovan Rossa that every visitor was required to address some verse or a stanza to Gaiscanaun or, if he didn't, the sea would be rough there on his passing it the second time. Diarmuid thought for a few moments and these are the words he uttered :

O white-breasted Gaiscanaun of the angriest current
Let me and all in this boat go past you in safety;
Stay calm and don't drown me my secret, beloved one,
And I'll give you my word that to Clear I'll never return.[6]

One of the crew in the mail-boat went to America afterwards to make his own way in the world like everyone else; and it was customary for the men of Cape Clear to go fishing when they arrived there. This man I'm talking about was out fishing on one occasion when a gale blew up on them and so, although Boston was their home port, they were forced to run in its lee for shelter in New York. When they went ashore they were cold and wet, and said that the best thing they could do was to have a drink, a drop of spirits that would warm them. Together they went to a tavern and entered a room there and sat at a table while the captain called for a drink for them. It was a man who came to serve them. As quickly as the one from Clear saw the man who came to serve them he recognised him; he knew that it was O'Donovan Rossa was there. He wanted to make himself known to him, and pondered how he would do it. He hit on the idea of reciting the verse about the Gaiscanaun and when Diarmuid heard it, his eyes revealed his bewilderment.

'Ah, indeed!' said he, 'as sure as I'm alive you are the son of Fineen from Cape Clear.'

'I am so,' the man replied.

'Musha you're welcome,' said O'Donovan Rossa. 'People meet but the hills and mountains never do!'

Their stomachs were too small for them for the rest of the time they were there : if they were to drink all the stock in the house he wouldn't take a farthing from them—for he was the owner of both the house and the pub.

And here's another story I heard my father telling : something that happened during the life of his grandfather from whom he

5

heard the story—a thing that occurred a couple of hundred years ago : he remembered a fine day when the wind was from the north-west that the royal cutter came from that point, from Castletownbere, bearing north-east of Clear and then out through the Gaiscanaun sound—it was on its way to Cork.

Young Morty O'Sullivan was being towed by a rope round his neck in the wake of the cutter, and he dead; and his two retainers were on board with bolts on their hands and feet on their way to be hanged in Cork. That was the sorry day in Clear when they saw the horrible treatment being given to Morty's corpse.[7] The women of the Island were weeping freely and for a long long time—and here is how the poet Dónal O'Connell, one of the attendants, sang his grief :

Morty Oge

Through Munster five times I would stride with you and over all lands,
—And even through the troops of the Prince—to get back to our people.
It was Puxley left us sad with the lashing of oppression,
In Cork bound in bonds with no hope of being freed.

O Great God of might I crave help and kind grace from You
The gallows tomorrow is before us with no hope of escape;
The ropes will be choking us 'mid the deafening roar of the mob;
Though he left us in their sway I pray the Great God for our master.

Dearest friend of my heart, O Morty, my belov'd and my treasure!
The ruffians exult that they've severed your bright head at last;
One day I saw you myself, a grand sword in your hand
With which you would slash a wide gap through the guard of King George.

If I were in Iveragh all the people would be keeping my wake,
And friars and priests would be chanting the Passion for me;

There's many a strong, sturdy man from Glencar to Ceann
     Bólus
Who grieves for our fate with no way of escape in our power.

Keep on praying for us Kerrymen : sweet and soft are your
     voices.
You'll always have my blessing though I'll never return alive,
For high on three spikes our heads will be a show for them all
Under the snow of the night and the woes of all weathers.

In Paris it was you gained the palm, and in Spain won a title;
From the Lady Clare came a fine lace array as your birthright;
You were a captain in charge of the guardsmen of the realm of
     France,
Yet nothing could please you but returning to Ireland—and
     death.

My woe and my heartfelt dismay that you came back to Ireland,
And that I ever saw you that day that you visited Béara,
Though you were the best captain and master that any man
     could have;
God grant that tomorrow our souls greet each other in glory!

In all my days' wandering your name and your fame knew no
     match
For your singing, your wisdom, your conduct, and excellent
     manners :
There's a maiden in London hoping day after day that you'll
     come
Very soon with your ships for the quips and debates she so
     craves.

I am pierced by a fierce burning grief that my people don't
     know
That we're held and condemned, and must die by next Friday—
If they did they would muster a crowd and find all that's
     required for our waking—
So there's an end to the story of Dónal, but pray evermore for
     his soul.[8]

7

CHAPTER TWO

'Learning is a hard thing, if how I
get it is the way the world gets it.'

I remember the first day I ever went to school. I was about five years of age. When a beginner starts school it is the custom to have an experienced person go along with him. Because I was the eldest of the family that meant that no one from our house was with me. But I recall that I was put in the care of a neighbouring young girl, for a short while, on my way to and from the school, until I became accustomed to the road and the people.

Only one thing worried me : I used to be really scared of a flock of geese on my way there. They are the greatest enemy the young have; and whenever I saw them I used have to jump in over the ditch and go a roundabout way until I would find myself rid of them. And indeed it's often one of them took a pinch at and a bite of the calf of my leg for I had neither brogue nor stocking on me. Peg Rishtard's big grey gander almost put an end to my life one day when he felled me in the mud; but as the luck of the world would have it a man named Seán Ó Muirithe came along the road from the west, and but for him the gander had me dead that day.

Well then!—The first day I entered the school the master called me up to him, and he enquired from me in English what name I had; but I didn't understand him. Then he asked me in Irish :

'*Cad is ainm duit?*' said he. I told him. 'And haven't you any English?' he added.

'No,' said I, 'not a syllable.'

'Well, little fellow, you'll have to throw away your Irish now and speak English from this out,' he went on.

At that time masters were required by law not to allow an word of Irish to be spoken in school. Yet the teacher himself had the Irish fluently. The nickname he had was 'The White-haired Master—with the broken leg', for the joint of one of his knees didn't work and, as a result, that leg was rigid—as stiff and straight as a stick.

8

He gave me a little book in English as a gift, a thing he did for every beginner. That was the book that took me a long time until I was able to master it in any way. It must have taken me a month to learn the first page in it, that is the A-B-C, for it was really hard work for me to change my language from the Irish to English.

And I remember another thing: there was a little frame in the school that had thin rods of iron across it from side to side with a dozen little balls on each one of them. The balls were black, and yellow, and white, and blue—they were every colour of the rainbow. The master used to give that frame to five or six of us at a time and tell us to keep counting the little balls in English, and it is we were busy handling it and passing on as speedily as we were able to. 'Twas often the White-haired Master stole up from behind us unawares to see what we were up to. And this is what happened one day: he was standing beind me and I was counting in this way—*aon, dó, trí.* I didn't know where I was when I got an almighty start from a blow of the back of his hand on my ear. I still remember what he said: 'TAKE THAT NOW!' I kept those three words he said in my head for, indeed, I had paid for them dearly at that moment.

I imagine the pay the master got from the Board at that time wasn't much to talk of for every garsoon had to bring him a penny as a week's fee every Monday morning; the one who hadn't the penny gave two hen-eggs, or a bottle of milk, or a sod of turf—for he lived in the school and so every sort of thing came in handy for him as well as the money. It was often he was bothered about his not being able to teach the pupils the English as well as he would like to. Then it was that he would begin to abuse them, and it was in the Irish he did so, for that was what they best understood; and so they remembered what he had to say. Like this he used to speak. 'I'm not a bit surprised the way ye are—upon my word, what am I to say? Ye are the way your people and ancestors were before ye; ye are like all those that went before ye; for ye will have the learning ye require: the line-fishing frame, the skills of fishing with line and hook. Ye'll go out in the boats and ye sitting on the tafts with a finger stretched out under the line over the upper strake

9

of the boat waiting for the bite of a fish.[1] That's the schooling ye prefer, and that's what ye'll have too!' And what he foretold came true, for when they were capable of going fishing that is what they did.

The custom of the Clear schoolboys at that time when they used to get an hour off for play—that is in summertime—was to go swimming in Tradoonclayreh. The journey there didn't take long—about ten minutes going and ten minutes back. Ah, I would like to be as light-footed today as I was at that time! When we returned from the swim we had other games to play until we were called in : the youngest of us played a game of buttons and the older boys quoits, and Irish was used for all our games.[2] It used to gladden our hearts to be outside the walls of the school and to be free to speak Irish to one another for, as quickly as we went in under the rafters of the schoolhouse we had to put aside our Irish and begin the hard work— that is the learning of English. In those days if anyone had a half a word of English the one who couldn't understand at all would say that that person was 'well-spoken, knowledgeable, and had a fluent flow of English.'

Whenever the master was expecting the coming of the inspector this is what he used say : 'Well, children, tomorrow is Big Bartholomew's day![3] Let me see you all in good heart and full of courage. Don't be a bit afraid of him! Do your best to see if I would gain anything good by ye, for if ye let me down I'll be penniless.' Then, turning to me : 'Don't forget to bring an armful of meadowsweet with you tomorrow to put in the corner there in the way that there will be a fragrant odour throughout the school before himself.' I would remember to do so, and he would give me a penny as a reward.

In those times there was no end to the young people's being taught the Catechism as soon as ever they went to school. As for myself I know that I didn't begin to learn it until after I had spent a year at school; and the master was a great hand at teaching it to us, although there was only a single book dealing with the whole subject. When the hours for school were behind us the class learning the prayers went to the chapel—it was only a short distance away, just a few perches of the road. The master used to read all the little book from cover to cover and leave each of us to memorise the amount he could manage during the time that it took. And so we continued like that, day after day, and as the time was passing we were always improving. Although we weren't able to write or read the Irish we were able to speak it, with fluent ease, and that is the reason that we were so skilled at learning the prayers by heart from the recitation of the master. I suppose it would be wondered at greatly if the young people of today were to learn the Catechism in English from the recitation of the teachers as we did sixty years ago.

After two or three months the priest came to visit us one day.

'Well, Master,' said he, 'how are the young ones doing in the prayers?'

'There's no reason to fault them, Father, seeing the shortness of the time that they're at them : they are doing very well,' was the master's reply.

'I'll come along to see you again in a week's time and ask them a few questions, and I'll know then how ye're doing,' said the priest.

He did as he said. He continued to visit us very often and as the time passed he was getting harder in his examination. Upon my word—to tell you the full truth—the one who couldn't answer him to his satisfaction was humble enough under the threat of his stick.

For two years, from one day to the next, we were learning the prayers until we were fit for Confirmation by the Bishop. The last week it was that we had the big examination by the priest, and he said that he would give a shilling to each of the four best of us. There were sixty-five in the class, taking boys and girls together. I myself was the youngest of the whole band, and ambasa I won a shilling. I was in high glee coming home with my prize.

The day came : a very fine one in midsummer, about the Feast of St John. Out to Baltimore we went by boat, that is a seven mile journey by sea. The Bishop used to come to Ráth Chapel, which was the parish church. We had a two mile walk to it from Baltimore. That was the first day ever that I set foot on the mainland.

We all met in Baltimore and it didn't take us long to reach

11

Ráth Chapel. There was only a short wait for us until the Bishop came—I recall that he was in a closed carriage with a pair of horses pulling it. We were all called into the chapel; and there were classes present from all parts of the parish but we were the only Irish-speaking one. The place where the Bishop sat was on a chair inside the rail at the foot of the altar. Every priest had his own class, and we ourselves were the first class the Bishop tested. I remember that he asked me only two questions which I still recall quite clearly; and I know what he said to me: *Imigh síos, tá san go maith.* After he had questioned all the young people he gave the crown of excellence to the Irish-speaking class from Clear.

After being confirmed I went to school again; but I only stayed there until the coming spring. I went no higher than 'the second book'. There was no cure for it for I had to stay at home to do a little bit of work and be of general use. That left me without schooling or knowledge and unable to write or read —and it was often since then that I regretted it. But there's no profit in private grief. I didn't understand myself in time, for an old head is never put on young shoulders.

CHAPTER THREE

My first trip to the market, and
the things I learned from Glavin.

At that time people had to begin the springtime farming work
early in the year, more especially any person who was short-
handed. As to ploughs and horses, there were no more than
three or four of them there, and that many didn't go far for the
rest of the people in the Island. Signs on it the men with the
spade had to begin the digging of the lea ground just on the
heels of Christmas. To turn the sod of a half-acre or three-
quarters of land with a spade was very hard work for a man on
his own, and sometimes he was a good bit behind-hand. They
used to make out that the man who had not planted the last of
his potatoes by the first fortnight of March would be in a bad
way from that time out. The spring is the busy, bustling time
of the year : it is also the time for sowing the wheat, and 'the
dark-moon of February' was deemed to be the proper time to
sow the grain.[1]

During that time I was able to help out a little, and it was
for that reason I was kept from school. I was all the more eager
to do anything I could when I got a hint that my father would
allow me to go to the fair with him in order to sell the pigs for
the summer. Although they were only raw, red banbhs at the
time, I used to be counting the days, for it seemed very long to
me till they would be fat. Puny scrawny creatures they were,
showing little sign of turning out well and there was no day that
I hadn't a knife and some old basket with me to cut and gather
dandelions for them because it has been said that, with the
exception of potatoes, they are the best feeding for pigs. I used
to blend Indian meal stirabout with them and sprinkle some
milk on the mixture, and that made a good meal for them;
they had been left entirely in my charge to take care of them.

One particular day I called them to their dinner and I
couldn't find a trace of them. I went looking for them and
searched high up and low down. Where should I find them,
late in the evening, but down on the strand, eating two sorts of
seaweed called *doolamaun* and *loke,* and they up to their bellies

13

out in the sea.[2] I drove them home, and indeed I didn't spare the rod on them. From that day until the one they were sold you could see them swelling and bursting with fat. I wonder was it the beating I gave them or that meal they had in the sea that did them such good.

Referring to the springtime again—the manuring of the potatoes used to be a great burden in Cape Clear at that time. There was no barn-manure worth talking about, and what there was of it would be used in the potato-plot; so, in order to finish the rest of that job we waited for the big tide in order to cut the *loke* which the people carried on their backs in baskets because donkeys were not as numerous in those days as they are now. That tells us that the poor people of this Island had a hard, irksome life during those days. But time was always passing quickly, and so the potato-field was manured and the first earthing done in April; from the middle of May on it was in need of the second earthing.

'If we had the second earthing finished,' said my father to me one day, 'we would be thinking of going to the fair on the Feast of St John.'

There were wings on my heart with delight when I heard talk of going to the fair. At the time we had a small little boat of our own, and that was the boat that was used to carry out the pigs. Three others of the neighbours, who had pigs too, went out along with us also for the fair.

In those times they had to leave home the day beforehand and spend that night in the town, for Skibbereen is fifteen miles from Cape Clear. It was their town for market, fair, and general business the one to which they travelled and from which they returned by boat. If the wind were against them they had to row the whole way; if they had a favourable wind the sail did the job.

Well that was the first day ever that I went to Skibbereen. Whatever person was in the boat then, or wasn't in it, there was a man in it whose name was Glavin. He was old and a polished, persuasive talker : it was said that during his day the one capable of excelling him could not be found in West Carbery. There was poetry in every word that came from his mouth. A

14

man of no great height, he was, however, extremely well-built and strong.

On our way up stream I was gazing at all the things I could see everywhere on the banks of the river, and asking the men what this was and that—everything looked so wonderful and strange to me.

'That's Kaynafeölah inside there,' said Glavin, 'and I'll tell you a story about it. A young fellow who had been fined for having drunk too much ran away to Cape Clear long ago, but the constables got a tip off of some sort, like one would get in "burn-the-cake", that he was in the Island. They followed him in, caught him, made him their prisoner, and were bringing him by boat to Skibbereen. That same day there was a stiff north-west breeze blowing so that the boat had a fair wind. There was a conspiracy between the man steering the boat and the young lad that the latter would be given a chance to jump ship in some suitable spot; and Kaynafeölah was the only place that that could be done, for the deep-water channel ran alongside it so that the boat could be brought in close there. And all went well : the lad was standing for'ard of the mast-taft on the lee side of the sail and, while the boat was passing the stone slipway, the young fellow leaped ashore and hid in a fissure in the rocks until the boat had disappeared from his sight. From the moment they left Cape Clear the constables had paid no attention to him, for they imagined that he had as little chance of leaving the boat as if he were actually in the prison. But ambasa, they made a foolish mistake; when they reached journey's end there wasn't trace or tidings to be got of the boyo.'

We were making good progress in the meantime. I saw a big well-sheltered wood with a mansion at its centre. You couldn't see much of it apart from glimpses of the chimneys between the trees. I asked Glavin what the place was, and he told me that it was called Creagh and that our lord in this world lived in the Big House I saw in the wood.[3]

'Lord of my soul, Glavin,' said I, 'that's a splendid dwelling-place he has!'

'Didn't you ever hear, child, what the poet said?'—and he sang *The Song of Treason* for us as follows :

15

The Song of Treason

Stretched last night on my bed and I rapt by the happenings in
    Ireland,
I bowed down in reverence to the Blessed Oil and the Sacred
    Body of Christ,
And acknowledged the Latin and the matchless commandments
    of God,
And the bright blessed Virgin who shines as the Queen of the
    saints.

Were I a wise writer fully skilled in matters of learning,
I would flawlessly tell all my tale which would certainly please,
How O'Connell made our countrymen trust in the might of
    God's grace
Who for ages were vagrants and shelterless strayed by the roads.

The damned and bold offspring of Calvin and Luther are harsh,
Those accursed authors who quickly gave in to the devil—
The savage infliction of pain is their game without ceasing :
Like mad rabid dogs, in June is their high point of menace.

Poor Ireland by them has been ripped and shred to thin ribbons;
In this life they have ceaseless comfort and ease unending;
At their every feast they have sweetmeats and dainties to eat :
Yet their bellies will be empty and we'll see them in direst need.

Their coaches are glowing in a glory of golden display;
On hills they plant woods to shelter themselves from the weather.
And to warm their bellies—while we pour out our sweat every
    day :
But never in life again will they see their present day's sway.

O bright blessed Virgin who pulls down the devils of hate,
Whose clean sword of defence is owned by God's Son of the
    graces,
Our Donal is forty, with the knave and the ace in his hand,
And if he wins the game the sway will be ours for all time.

Stand stoutly your ground and do not be lacking in courage :
The due time is finished and quickly they'll yield way to us;
For all this life's span only lasts a very short spell,
While the kingdom of heaven to us is promised by the Father
    and Son.[4]

He had only sung that much by the time we reached Old
Court, and I interrupted him by enquiring about the castle
there, and whether he had any story about it.[5]

'I have musha,' he said. 'Although I myself don't recall it,
but only in so far as I heard it. There was a mansion there in
olden times where a gallows was sited on which the noose was
put round the throat of many a son of a good father and
mother for little cause. And do you see this wood nearer to
you?'

'Yes,' I answered.

'There's an ancient curse on that wood,' he went on.

'Why so?' said I.

'Well,' said he, 'there's an orchard in that wood, and I heard
that a child—the only one his mother had—plucked an apple
there and was condemned to be hung as a result. From that
day forward no apple grew in that same orchard.'[6]

'Twas shortly afterwards that we passed a graveyard on the
northern bank of the river.

'That is the graveyard called Abbeystrewery Monastery,' he
said, 'and I heard a strange story about it—if it is true. It has
been said that that monastery was being built first on the other
side of the river. After the first day's work everyone went home
for the night; but wasn't it they were astonished when they
came in the morning to continue their work : what had been
done the previous day had been shifted to where you see the
place now. They said to one another that it was a miracle, and
that it must be that it was ordained that they should build it
there. So there it stands now on the sunny side.'[7]

In a few minutes more we were at the quay by the central
bridge of the town. While we were coming alongside the quay,
there were strangers standing on it.

'Do you think they are butchers?' one of the men in the boat
asked another.

17

'I think they are so,' he answered.

'Well, if so,' said the first one who spoke, 'there's some stir in the pig market today, and let us not be too soft with them.'

They were right. No sooner had the end of the rope been twisted around and tied to the post than they jumped into the boat to us, and there wasn't a moment's delay by them in buying all the pigs on board with the people who owned them quite pleased with the result of their bargaining.

We stayed in the town that night. Lodgings were booked in the house in which they were always accustomed to stay. When the night came on everyone made his way to the lodging-house We all ate our suppers together, and then went off to sleep.

But I myself, at any rate, didn't sleep well. I heard the market clock striking twelve, and 'twas shortly after that I heard the shriek outside in the street.

'O, Mary Mother,' I said, 'who was it that left the howl out of him?'

'Arooh,' said one of the men, 'that's the town crier, and every hour the clock strikes he'll pass through the streets of the town calling out loudly in that way until the bright dawn of tomorrow. And now, child, don't utter another word for the rest of the night, and be up early so that you can see the big coach before it sets out for Cork.'

We rose at eight o'clock in the morning. Everyone had some business to do before they would all go home. Having had our breakfast, each one paid his bill to the woman of the house before he left and bade her farewell with a blessing on her.

When we went out on the street I asked Glavin where I could see the big coach.

'It isn't far from us,' he replied, 'there it is yonder outside the door of the Post Office.'

I went over to look at it. There it stood with four horses tackled to it, one pair ahead of the other. I noticed that they were prancing like dancers on the road; all that was wrong with them was the delay before they got the freedom of their feet. With all the clatter and chatter it was the most stirring day I had seen up to then. I imagined that all the people living in Ireland were in the town that day. If a yellow brass pin were to fall from the air you would think that it would land on someone's head. When all the mail had been loaded on the coach the passengers followed suit and mounted—and off they went. I can tell you that it was a long journey from there to Cork.[8]

In the twinkling of an eye all the people had scattered, each one attending to his own affairs, and we were thinking about making for home as quickly as there was enough water to float the boat.

'Here now men,' said my father, 'let you all have your traps and your gear brought to the boat about one o'clock as the tide will be high enough then for us to leave. As the breeze is from the north-west we'll have a fair wind home, and when we will be below the bridge we'll stand our mast and set our sail.'

They were ready at the time agreed and we started out on the way after drinking a *deoch an dorais*. We had all the fair wind we wanted, and it took us only two hours to get home and land at Foilcoo strand.

When I reached the house I had as many stories to tell as a sailor who would be after going round the world. And, as for the night, when I went to bed I didn't sleep a wink; for I still imagined that I could hear the town-crier calling out loudly outside, and the sounds of horses and trucks were in my ears.

CHAPTER FOUR

That time long ago when I was
'on my own catch' among the men.[1]

There was a lot of small fishing boats attached to the Island at that time. Rowing boats they were—some four-oared and others six-oared—and a crew in them in accordance with the size of the boat. Anyone who didn't have a boat used to fish in his neighbour's. Bream was the most abundant of the fish that could be caught although there were other sorts fished for as well, such as gurnet, scad, pollock, and 'connor'. And, then, when the year was drawing to an end the hake used to come inshore, and they did very well fishing for those too.

They used to begin fishing those smaller varieties of fish at the beginning of June, for none were to be found until then. By that time their potato-plots were in good trim and various jobs at home off their hands. During the whole of the winter and spring the boats were beached well up on the grassy banks above the strands until the due time came. When the day came to launch each owner had by then provided a crew for his boat : five men at the very least in some of them, and up to seven in more. Then they were launched, and the fishing that followed was often cold, wet, hungry and dreadfully hard work; unless you were on the watch-out early and late you wouldn't have anything as a result of your toil.

I remember the very first day I went fishing. I was 'on my own catch' in one of the boats for neither I nor other young lads of my like were able to catch a man's share of fish; that is why beginners were 'on their own catch'. On the evening before we started the owner of the boat gave us strict orders not to sleep it out in the morning because there would be a grand timely tide out at the very tip of the point of Illaunbrock with the early dawn, 'and I have a feeling that each of us will kill a fine strap of fish.'

'A master's order is always absolute.' We were up with the first light of day when the clouds were just tinged with red, and we made no great delay for our boat was ready and moored in the cove throughout the night. All we had to do was let go the rope, jump on board, and set off. It took us no more than ten minutes pulling with our four oars to reach the fishing ground. We anchored there, and no sooner had we the lines out than the fish were biting, and so we were hauling in exhausted bream until we had made a catch of four hundred in that place. I put a concealed, secret mark on every one of the fish I got so that I would be able to identify all that were mine when the whole catch was being shared out on the strand.

It was a fine calm morning; indeed it would gladden anyone to be in a boat. But with the sun up in the south by that time, the hunger was nagging me and the day wearing me out: there's no stamina in young people in comparison with men; indeed it seemed an eternity until I was at home for my breakfast. 'A child's appetite or a hen's craw,' as the proverb goes.

When the tide turned on us the fish shut their mouths, and then it was that we landed. The catch was thrown out on the strand and I picked out my own. Six shares were made of the rest, that is, a share for each of the five men and one for the boat. When the heaps were ready lots were drawn. One of the men bent down and picked a white little pebble up from the strand. 'That's my choice for drawing the lots,' he said. Another chose a 'blister' of doolamaun for himself, and another a shell, and still another a little bit of weed; and so on in the way that no two men chose alike. All these were placed in the hands of the first man who spoke. He then turned his back to the rest of them so that they couldn't see what he was doing. What he did was hide them in his fists as he pleased. He turned around to face them once more and said : 'I have three lots in each hand. Now Seán name them!'

'Let the one closest to the thumb of your right hand begin,' said Seán, 'and take that share up there, and so on as they go from that down.'

He opened his fist and threw the lot first called down on the first share of fish, the second on the one closest to it, and the lot in the heel of his hand on the third share. The three men who drew those heaps lifted them up straightaway. Then Seán spoke again : 'Let the one closest to the thumb of your left hand have that share below there to the south and so on from that up.' Everyone knew his own portion so that no one could show by the look of his mouth that he was dissatisfied when he had the fruit of the lot he himself chose.

But whenever they were in a hurry they had a quick way to share out the fish. When the catch was being divided into heaps one of the men kept his back to the work afoot. Another picked up half-a-dozen stones from the strand and threw one of them down on one of the heaps asking in the meantime : 'Who is to have that?' The man with his back turned to them answered and said. 'Let you yourself take it.' He then threw a stone on a second heap and said : 'Who is to have this?' The man looking away answered : 'Let it be mine.' So the drawing of lots continued until the business was finished and everyone took his share of the fish away to his home with him.

It was usually the women who washed and gutted the fish and put them on salt—that is pickled them—for in those times they had great experience entirely of the work.

The fishermen used to have great fishing and make fine catches the weeks when the tides were getting big, for that made the fish bite very freely. But during the days of the spring tide the fish act just as if they were sick : they have no inclination to bite and won't take any kind of bait. But not so the fisherman : it is never convenient for him to be tired; he has to be out fishing at all times whether he catches anything or not—for the winnings from the sea are not always heavy.

During the months of June and July the weather used to be so fine that there was no need for them to draw the boats up at night; they simply moored them in the coves. They had particular ones of these coves for that purpose where the boats were always left afloat—that is Coosadooglish, Coosanvaud, Coosheen-Foile-Rónaun, or the one at Illaun Beg in Doonclayreh. But from the first day of August out the boats were beached every single night and launched again in the morning; throughout a long autumn night they had no confidence that it wouldn't blow.

During the period that they were engaged in fishing they used to go once a fortnight, or once every three weeks, at the very longest, to the market with their fish—and Skibbereen was the market town they had then. Hucksters met them on the quay, and they wouldn't make much delay in taking their catch off

22

their hands, for there was a great demand for fish at the time—whatever about the way things stand today. The country people were just as eager to get the fish from the hucksters, for in those days people were hungrier for fish than they are today.

As the unfortunate people of the Island had to spend sparingly so that they would be able to pay the rent at the close of the year, they didn't waste one penny they earned, although they were often in dire need. The great majority of them had a small patch of land each, but even so, it was little they made out of it. In all truth but for the pennies they earned from the fishing they wouldn't be able to pay the rent, it was so big a burden on them. The landlord was quite unconcerned about where they got it or how they made it provided he was paid his rent; and that same person would give them no quarter but, throw them out on the roadside if they hadn't paid the rent by St Stephen's day. Yes, indeed, they used have to knuckle down to it in earnest throughout the year in order to have the rent collected : the old proverb reveals the hard choice—'Rent for the landlord or food for the child.'[2]

That was the kind of life the people of Cape Clear led when I was a quite hardy young child. No one had the second pair of boots to put on his feet nor the second trousers to cover his bones, and they toiled day and night trying to rear their families and to meet their small expenses by every means possible. The very ground knows that it was a hard life trying to make a living then; but still people had to be satisfied : they never experienced anything else.

But I'll get back to myself. After being the first year 'on my own catch', from that out I was able to play my own part and, so got my full share with the other men. For it isn't strength or dexterity alone that helps one to kill fish but a native cuteness and good judgement. Even though I say it myself I was as handy and fortunate with a fishing line as anyone in the boat.

When the autumn was well advanced the hake came to the fishing grounds. We used then give over catching the smaller varieties and go after the hake, for a hundred of them brought in more money than seven hundred bream. They are an entirely different sort of fish : 'green-fish' is what they are called; and

23

there is no fish in the water that is grander to eat than they are, whether fresh or salted.

At that time fish were sold by number, and the mode of counting meant that sixty pair made a count of a hundred fish, and as well as that four pair were thrown in as a small addition.[3]

I recall one particular year that there was no demand for fish in the markets. When the gale day came for paying the rent more than a good half of them hadn't the wherewithall to pay it : their fish remained on their hands that year. There was no cure for it but to make the best of things by giving the fish to the landlord in place of the rent. He took their offer in good part : he accepted the fish and gave them a clear bill for the year.

'Well,' as one man said to another, 'fish are as good as money : we have a guarantee of the shanty for another year at any rate. There's no knowing how God will come to our aid next year.'

'You're right there,' said the other man, 'God is the generous One, when people are "in tight corners".'

CHAPTER FIVE

Fishing with the Big Boats

About fifty-four years ago, when I was about fifteen years old, rumours were abroad in Cape Clear that there were big boats fishing out of Kinsale and that they were catching mackerel; the earnings from them were big, for there was a great demand entirely for that fish in the market on the other side, that is the English market. That sort of boat couldn't be got anywhere except in the Isle of Man at that time; and it was difficult to obtain one of them for they cost far too much. One fresh from the stocks, with all that went with her, cost £600.

There was another kind of boat available which was far from newly-built, and they could be got cheaply : with all the gear included, their price was about a couple of hundred pounds.[1] Two men from the Island went into partnership, journeyed over, bought one of this second kind I just mentioned, and brought her home. They fished for a season with her and did so well that during the second year the Island wasn't dependent on one only but actually had four of them. Indeed they were doing so well that no one had any regard for the old boats any more. Then they began to get the new boats mentioned above built on contract for themselves. It was quite a problem to arrange the matter but this is how they used to do it : they found guarantors, went to the bank and raised some of the money, and then made up the balance between themselves.

Each of these big boats had an eight man crew, and every one of them was just as good as a dwelling-house. Their keels were 45 ft in length, and they had a beam of 15 ft and a depth of 12 ft. Every one of them had two masts with four sails on the foremast—which was the main one. This was from 53 ft to 59 ft in height. The small, or mizen-mast had only one sail.

Beneath deck each boat was divided into four 'rooms', the cabin—which was a fine cosy place, being aft. It had bunks for eight, and a cupboard that held a week's stock of food, a kettle and pot, as well as eight plates and eight cups. The clock and compass were also kept there. Everything in the cabin was equally accessible and handy, even the fresh water which came

25

from a water-cock. All one had to do was to put the kettle under it to fill it when one wanted to put it on the fire. And as for the fire-grate it was splendid; it wouldn't take long to boil a kettle.

The 'room' for'ard of the cabin and closest to it held the nets, and it was separated from the cabin by a strong partition. That 'room' was large enough to hold forty-five nets. In a corner of it was a big iron container in which was kept the week's supply of water for the crew. A pipe stretched from this through the partition and as far as the tap in the cabin.

Beyond that was the hold for storing the fish, and it was large enough to take eight or nine thousand mackerel. The space closest to the prow, and so for'ard of the hold, was used for the ropes. It held twelve coils of rope each one being a hundred and twenty fathoms long. All that rope was neatly coiled and bound.

The whole boat was decked in such a way that no water could enter anywhere except through the entrances which had hatches that were placed on them or lifted according as the work on board required.

Altogether there were twenty-five of these new boats in the Island, and I myself, fished in one of them in former years. Better still the fish were plentiful and to be found close at hand; and Baltimore, so much closer to us than Skibbereen, was at that time the place for marketing the fish. Buyers came from England to purchase the fish, and however plentiful they were the buyers couldn't get enough—although there were four to five hundred boats fishing out of Baltimore. I often saw three steamers being filled in a single day for the English market which is proof that the fish was in great demand over there.

We used to start preparations for this kind of fishing in the beginning of March. It took over a week to make one of these boats ready for sea. First of all the nets were brought from home to the harbour to be barked in cutch before they were put aboard the boat, for otherwise they would rot. The boats were painted from the keel to the upper strake, and the spars were scraped clean and oiled, so that everything would be shipshape for the season. Then the train of nets and all the rope were put on board.

26

When everything was in proper order the captain used to say : 'Well, boys, let every man of you bring the makings of his bed on board tomorrow, for we'll have Mass before we leave the harbour.' We did that; and so everyone brought his 'shake-down' with him and put it in his bunk. As well as having his own bunk each member of the crew had a locker of his own for his clothes and all his personal things.

We were all aboard early in the morning, and the priest came and said Mass in the cabin. When the Mass was over he used to bless a bucket of water and he handed a holy-water sprinkler; and we got down on our knees on the deck so that he could bless us first with the holy-water, and then the nets, the ropes, and every part of the boat—and then he himself gave us his blessing for the season.

We sailed out then until we were twelve miles from land, and not ourselves alone for a large number of boats besides ours was there also. We had to give each other a clear berth—that is the length of a train of nets—or else we would shoot down on one another, which was a bad turn for a fisherman to do to another.

The captain who was at the helm gave an order then : 'Boys, we are at our berth! Everybody on deck to prepare for shooting! Stand by the halyards! Lower the mainsail and stow it by the side!'

No sooner was it said than done. Everyone jumped up to attend to his own job : the hatch was lifted from the nets and two men caught hold of one end of the train; another man kept an eye on the rope for fear any tangle would come in it. Still another stood for'ard of the foremast in order to raise or lower the forestay sail according as headway would be required by the boat.

They used then call to the man in the foredeck and say : 'Raise that sail a little!' This was done straightaway. 'She has headway : shoot them in the name of God!' When the two men who had a hold of the head of the train between them cast it into the sea, they used to say : 'May ye prosper greatly!'

Shooting the nets was a task that took three-quarters of an hour; and I can tell you that there was sweat in their boots by the time the last was out. Then the boat was brought to, head

27

into the wind. The long rope mentioned already, and another called the swing rope which was tied in an eye at the end of the train of nets were run through the hawse in the stem of the boat, and the two ropes were attached to firm cleats especially set aside for them. Yes! the nets were catching fish then. The mizen sail was raised and that kept the boat steady with her head into the wind. Close to the stern of the boat a strong crutch was set up, and the mainmast, with all the blocks, shrouds, and halyards belonging to it, was seated on this crutch that had been prepared for it. Then the tackle from the mast was placed in different parts of the boat in order to keep it secure when she was rolling and wallowing in the sea.

They also had a punt on board, and there was a special place on the port side for it so that it would not be in the way of the work when the nets were being hauled. That left the starboard of the boat clear and uncluttered from stem to stern; for it was from that side that the nets were always cast—and I myself heard a story about that custom. In the days of the old law when the Apostles used to be fishing the nets were let out on the port side. One particular day they were on board the boat and the Lord told them to go out fishing. They said that they were exhausted from fishing and had caught nothing. 'Try once again,' He said, 'and shoot your nets from the starboard.' They did so, and the nets filled up so much with fish that they couldn't pull them on board. From that day to the present one nets are cast from the starboard side of every boat. And that then is the reason why the old fishermen used to say: 'Let us shoot our nets in the name of Jesus, just as Peter did.'

At night-time a lantern was lit and hung from the forked point of an eight foot long iron spike which was placed standing in its proper position. During the night the safety of the boat and all in her depended on the light.

All that done we had our supper and afterwards prayers—that is to say 'Mary's Crown' or, as it is called in English, the Rosary. All but two men used then go to bed; although—to tell the truth—fishermen get little chance of rest or repose at sea apart from two or three hours if the night is fine. On the other hand if it looked threatening they set about hauling immediately after their supper.

28

At twelve o'clock the man on watch would call those who were asleep and tell them it was time to start hauling. We got up then and went on deck. Four of the men attended to the nets, that is two hauling them into the boat, and the other two stowing them in the hold. Those four had to put on suits of clothes that didn't let a drop of water in : they were made of oiled baffity, and every fisherman had an outfit of that sort for use if he needed it.[2]

For'ard was a capstan, with a thick barrel, which was attached to the mast-casing. Three turns of the long rope stretching out from the boat were twisted round that barrel, which had two bars or levers inserted in it at opposite sides. Two of the men manned one of these levers, and another one of them the other. That meant that seven of the crew were occupied, the eighth was in the rope-room below deck to hold the rope when it was played in to him, and to coil it at the same time.

It used to take them at least three hours to haul the train of nets on board, and you can take it from me that that was no easy, carefree job; on the contrary it was sheer slavery. But it has always been said that the man who has a profitable end in view never grows weary : if the nets were bright with fish that sight would give them greater zest for the work.

When we had the last one in we had to raise the mast and set the sail, and that was a very dangerous task as we poked about in the dark—only that every man was skilled at his own particular part of the job. Once under sail we headed for the fish-market in Baltimore.

At that time there were a dozen companies from Ireland and England that were represented in Baltimore by buyers who purchased the fish from the boats. These used to get vessels loaded with ice to come from Norway. These were unloaded and the ice was transferred to old hulks that had seen the last of their days at sea, and it was kept there for use during the season whenever it was required.

They also had wooden boxes each of which held a couple of a 'hundred' mackerel. Some of the ice was placed on top of the fish in the boxes and strong, firm covers nailed on the boxes in order to bring them over to the English market. It was often that I saw three steamers being filled as a result of one night's fishing by the fleet of boats; and, after all that, there was such a demand for fish over there that they couldn't get half of what they wanted.

But the boats weren't able to go fishing every night : if there was a calm night there was also its contrary. The boats used often keep beating about on the coast seeking shelter for shooting and, after it all, they would be nervous about doing so when it was blowing too hard. They used to forget about fishing that night and sail for the harbour closest to them. On such an occasion one of the crew would say to another one : 'The man who sleeps never lost it!' That is the way things were with the fishermen throughout the season : the fine night at sea and the bad night ashore; although they were often caught napping there was no cure for it when it happened but to do their best.

I remember one special night when we were after shooting not far from the Fastnet Rock. There had been a light fog and drizzle of rain when we shot the nets and, so we didn't leave them out long because we were afraid that it would blow : and that fear was fulfilled. The wind swung round to the north and blew really hard. You can be sure that we had black weals on our hands in the morning by the time we had hauled the nets on board and got the boat moving under a short sail; for the sails had to be reefed whenever there was a sharp wind and a high sea. To reach the harbour that morning we had to tack again and again because we were heading straight into the eye of the wind. You may well say that it was many the shower of spray that swept over us that day : wherever the sea struck us between the two eyes we were as blind as a hen at night for five minutes before we got our sight back again.

Such a day was harder on a man than a fortnight's fishing in fine weather. When the salt-water used to dry on a man's face you would think that it was the colour of snow. As fishermen say: 'A short sail makes a grey head'—that is turns a man's hair grey before its time.

By the end of June the season had finished, and the nets were landed, dried, and brought home. They then prepared for fishing with long lines, that is for catching fish found on the hard-bottom : ling, cod, hake, eels, skate, and halibut. This lasted for three or four weeks, and during that period we used to come home once a week with our catch in order to salt it while it was fresh because if it were 'soudy', that is stale, it wouldn't be tasty to eat. When it was brought home it was cured in airtight vessels containing pickle. After being eight days in the vessels it was taken out and washed in fresh water in order to get rid of the pickle. It was then left out in the sun until it was dry and fully cured, and after that it would last inside for seven years. It made grand seasoning for the potatoes in those days unlike that savourless stuff we get over from England at this present time which is so tough you couldn't pull it asunder.

After three or four voyages spent in that kind of fishing the season for the big boats ended for that year. All through the season the crew of each boat was almost like a family. They lived together in unbroken harmony without anyone charging another with lying or trying in any bitter way to best him in an argument; instead everyone attended to his own business as best he could.

We used to spend August in preparation for a second season —the autumn fishing : and that was a kind of fishing that was more profitable for and beneficial to the Island than was the fishing in the big boats. The kind I am referring to now was done close to their homes. There is a large extensive bay between the Island and the mainland, called Roaring Water Bay. In the autumn that used to fill up with mackerel, and at the time there were three score of open boats leaving Trakieran in search of these fish, with three men in each boat. When the season began every one of these craft used to put down six wooden anchors, of their own design and making in order to mark their berths. 'Killigs' they were called, and each of them contained a large stone weighing from a hundred and fifty to two hundred stones, so that they would keep their hold on the bottom-ground. From each of these anchors a rope stretched to the surface, and a ten-gallon keg was tied to the end of each rope to act as a buoy that remained constantly afloat on the surface of the water; and to avoid any confusion everyone had the number of his own boat on the kegs.

All the boats used to leave the harbour with the first yellowing of the sun in the afternoon, tie nets to every buoy and return to the harbour leaving the nets out until morning to catch the fish. I myself had one of these small boats at that time, and, just like everyone else, I made good pickings while the business lasted.

It was for the American market that those fish were cured and, by the by, they couldn't get enough of them for there was a tremendous demand for them in the western market.

With the coming of dawn the boats were out hauling the nets. When they had the last net aboard they returned to the harbour where five dealers were waiting on the quay and no sooner was each boat in than the fish was bought by the buyer who offered the highest penny for it. They used to be outbidding one another in this way until the very last boat arrived laden with fish.

When the fish were put ashore from the boats, each buyer ordered the team of handlers he had to work : some of them to cut the fish open with knives, others to gut them, and the rest to carry them from the trestle tables in baskets in order to throw them into a vat full of water for washing before putting them in pickle. They were then put into barrels which contained salt, and when the day's catch was packed into these strong pickle was sprinkled on it. After a week the fish was salted a second time, and then an air-tight cover was inserted in the rabbett or groove in the top of the barrel and secured in that position with the help of an iron hoop. Each barrel was then turned on its side and an auger-hole made in it; that was the bung-hole which was left open since it was essential to pour a drop of pickle into it every day during the period that they remained on the quay. When the day came for taking them away timber bungs were hammered into the openings in the sides.[3]

There wasn't a woman, a girl, or a child in the Island who couldn't earn something in those days; and there was often so much to do that the very fishermen themselves had to lend a helping hand when there were large landings of fish, for the sake of finishing the day's work.

That occupation, which I have just described, lasted for some twenty seasons. That was the time that Cape Clear had its largest fleet of boats; never before then or since was it so independent. It would sadden the person who had experience of that work if he were to visit the harbour today; all the bustle of the activity that was then utterly gone, and nothing at all to be seen but the cold and empty quays.[4]

CHAPTER SIX

The night of the Southern Gale, and the resulting misfortunes.

On the Monday night of the 25th of April, 1894, all the boats went to sea.[1] The Cape Clear fleet, always at home from Saturday to Monday, sailed from Trakieran that day. The boats from Baltimore set out from the harbour likewise and that evening was a really bad-looking one. Men were saying to one another that no nets would be shot that night or, if they were, that the night would be remembered yet for a long time.

The wind was south, south-west, and mast-high swells were breaking everywhere on the coast. They all spent the evening tacking and hugging the shore for shelter, in order to be within easy reach of the harbour if they were caught out—for they were afraid of the weather's worsening during the night. That fear was wellfounded.

On the boat in which I was we were arguing the toss among ourselves about whether we should shoot or not; and I have no doubts but that the same sort of dialogue was taking place on every boat in the fleet that evening. When it was getting very late one of the crew said that the night wouldn't be good and that it would be as well for us to head for the harbour.

'I don't know,' said the captain; 'by the tail-end of twilight we will have a full ebb-tide and the moon will be rising, and so perhaps the night will soften.'

Answering him another man said, 'Don't you see how bad it looks with that dark blue colour in the sky? It was never seen looking worse; and if it is fated to live up to its appearance, cut this ear off me if someone doesn't have a new tale to tell tomorrow, for don't you know well that there is no gale worse than the one that comes with the rising moon?'

The next man to speak said : 'There's a boat out there in the middle and she's shooting her nets; it is little fear of the night they have.'

' 'Tis just as well for us to take our chance with them too,' said the captain. 'Lower that sail quickly, and shoot them.'

Within five minutes the whole fleet was casting their nets :

34

they spurred and egged one another on just as when a sheep enters the pen the rest will follow it.

When the water changed colour with the ebb and the last of the twilight, the rising moon's light could be seen; but, even so, instead of thinking about calming, 'twas blowing it was.

'I'm afraid,' the captain said, 'that we have a troublesome night before us so, as soon as we have eaten our supper, we will knuckle down to work at once.'

No sooner had we drunk a cup of tea and eaten a few biscuits than we put on our oilskins and went straight up on deck for everyone to set to work, and with twice the usual effort having to be made by them as a result of the night's being so really bad. I myself was doing the work of two men for my partner had to leave me and go for'ard to help the three men who were pulling in the rope. That left me all alone hauling in the nets, and it was many a savage jerk I suffered from them before I had the tail-end buoy of the train on board. By that time there wasn't a shred of skin on my fingers; and what should cause that but the high sea tugging and tearing them through my gripping fingers as I was trying to hold them, not knowing what minute I would be swept overboard.

No sooner was that much done than the boat swung around in the weather—the wind on its beam and the sea on its side, so that she was like a cow wandering the road with the result that you would think it unnatural for a cat to keep its footing on the deck. We hoisted the leg of mutton trysail, that is the smallest sail we had on board, and her stem was turned towards land in the direction of the harbour—for we knew where it lay from us, according to the compass. When our prow pointed towards the harbour we were running small before the wind.

After being a half-an-hour under way we began to say to one another that it was calming a little. It was my responsibility and that of my partner on duty-watch to bring the boat into harbour—the others had turned in because of the softening that came at the time.

It was my partner who was steering and he told me to put the kettle on and make the tea, and when I had drunk a cup to come on deck to steer and let himself go below. 'Fair enough,' said I.

The kettle wasn't long boiling for there was a mighty fire under it. While I had the tea drawing I put a couple of eggs to boil in a saucepan. 'I'll be on deck with you in a few minutes,' I shouted to the man above.

The last word wasn't out of my mouth when he shrieked at me : 'For God's sake hurry on deck and lower the sail or the mast will be carried away any minute.'

I rushed up the ladder, released the halyard from the peg, and lowered the sail with a thud in a single movement. 'Well,' said my partner, 'she's much easier now.'

From one glance I gave towards the stern I saw that moment a startlingly bright 'sheegwee' coming across the water, heading for the boat.[2] 'Joseph,' I said. 'I'm afraid that we've seen the best of the night!'

'I think so,' he answered. 'Go below and rouse the rest of them.'

When I entered the cabin isn't it I was surprised to find my kettle of tea upside down and not a drop in it; the couple of eggs I left after me on the fire gone too, they and the ashes mixed together in a mess.

I told them to get up, that it was blowing fiercely entirely, and that we would be fortunate if we could make the harbour. We all went up on deck together; and I assure you that it wasn't food or drink, sleep or rest that we were bothering about but fully occupied with handling the boat as best we could, hoisting a scrap of sail on her from time to time to pluck her from the following seas; and sometimes, because of the strength of the wind, we had to haul it down and let her run before the wind, her poles stripped bare.

It wasn't too long before we raised the light at the harbour's entrance. The mouth of Baltimore Harbour was more dangerous than the coast outside for the water was light there, and some-times broke from the very bottom. But, God be thanked, while we were running in through it we ourselves hit a calm spell.

At that time the first yellowing of dawn was there. A few other boats entered the harbour along with us, and none of us stopped until we reached a fine calm inlet where wind wasn't lashing or sea tossing us. We put down two anchors, and tied ropes ashore from them also so that we could well sleep in peace; although it wasn't asleep we went but kept watching the boats coming in to see if all our neighbours would escape safe and sound.

About two or three hours after we had come in two of us went ashore. The first news we heard was that a boat had gone down in the harbour's mouth, she and all who were in her, without a man surviving who could tell the tale. God save all those where these tidings are told! The boat lost came from Newry in County Down.

But while some of the boats had still not come in, the gale hadn't yet reached the height of its fury. During the day they were arriving one after another, and it was at two o'clock in the evening that the very last boat reached Baltimore Harbour that day. Some of them ran for shelter to Castlehaven and Kinsale.

The captain and I were standing on the pier when that last boat came in at two o'clock with a bit of a sail that had been torn into tatters by the gale hanging from its mast. There was a full tide up to the tops of the quays at the same time. The man at the helm ran her in by the side of the quay without a thought of stopping her for he appeared to be unaware of what he was doing; that wasn't to be wondered at after what had happened to him before that. He would have smashed her into tiny splinters that very moment against the wall ahead of him were it not that two men on board a French fishing vessel moored to the quayside jumped aboard her while she was passing by, each with a rope in his hand; they brought her to a stop and tied her up alongside their own boat. There wasn't a man on her who was able to lend a hand in any way.

I myself and the captain boarded her. She was from the Isle of Man. We noticed that she had no punt on her, but that a part of her bulwark had been shattered and swept away. Another thing we took note of was that she had a crew of fleshy, lumpish old men, except for one young man aged about twenty-six years. We enquired what happened to them, and this young man told us that she shipped water as they were heading for the harbour from the south-west. Everyone of them took a firm hold of something to support himself, and one man gripped the punt. That sea swept the punt away and along with it the man who was holding firmly on to her. At the same time it smashed and carried off the bulwark of the big boat from the deck up. It was the captain's brother who was swept overboard and when he found out, as he steered the boat, that his brother was gone, he all but collapsed and died. He lost his hold on the helm, and the boat came to beam on to the sea. 'I caught hold of the tiller,' said the young man, 'and got her on course again before the weather; and but for the speed with which I did so we were all lost. I didn't let the tiller out of my fist until I brought her in here where she lies now. We lost all our nets from the nose out; and now as I'm alive I'm off to the pub, and I'll have a drop of spirits to warm myself for I'm sorely in need of it.'

When we had got all the day's news we went back aboard our own boat. The rest asked us what stories we had heard ashore and we told them what was after happening, and that all our own Island boats—apart from two—were safe in the harbour, and that the two others were in Castlehaven. We slept soundly that night; we were in need of it, and so in our sleeping we added part of the next day to the night.

The first one who got up in the morning went on deck and looked about him. 'I think lads,' he said when he returned to the cabin, 'that you can stay in your berths for what remains of the week : it's as bad-looking and threatening today as it was yesterday.' We gave that day and the coming night there, and on Thursday morning it was softening and calming. The gale had spent itself.

'We'll go home in the evening if we can,' said the captain, 'for all the people there are anxious because they don't know whether their own folk are dead or alive.'

At two o'clock in the evening we heaved the anchors and set our sails. As we were going out the harbour's mouth it was as calm as a lake. The person who had seen that place on Tuesday morning could not believe that it would ever again be so tranquil.

'Unlucky is the one who is lost in the tempest for the sun comes after the rain,' said I, remembering the proverb.

'That has been said,' remarked one of the others, 'and indeed it's grief for him too.'

When we were reaching in past Cooslahan Point at the eastern end of Cape Clear there was a man standing on the top of the cliff, and he shouted at the very top of his voice enquiring if everyone was alive after the gale. He was answered and told that all the Cape Clear boats were safe and sound.

That was the first report that reached the Island. As soon as I stuck my head inside the door my mother welcomed me: 'We thought,' she said, 'that we would never again see anyone who was out from among us. Have you any account of your brothers? Are they alive?'

'They are,' I answered; 'and the boat Tomás is in is on her passage home, and so he'll be here himself very shortly.'

'Thanks be to God,' she said, 'that everyone is safe. One can find something to take the place of everything but that of a human being.'

My father asked me what time we reached Baltimore Harbour that morning.

'Musha,' I said, 'just with the rising sun.'

'Arooh,' he replied, 'the weather wasn't at its worst at that time. And what time was Tomás in?'

'About eleven o'clock.'

'If it was at eleven that the *San Columba* came in all the members of her crew saw truly terrifying sights.'[3]

'They did,' said I, 'and according to what I heard tell they went very close to being lost at the harbour's mouth.'

When Tomás came in the first question I myself asked him was: 'What kept ye so late in reaching the harbour that day? Ye must have been very far out to sea.'

'About twenty miles,' he said.

'I suppose ye were a long way off to the lee?'

'We were,' said he, 'for the course we were steering was nor' nor'-west.'

'And when did ye make the last haul?'

'At eight o'clock,' he replied.

'Did ye hoist the mainsail at all?'

'No,' he said, 'but we had it ready for hoisting if we were caught out. We spread it over the hatches for fear the sea would take them. We were doing well until we got within a half-mile of the entrance. I can tell you that at the time we were right in the thick of the storm with every sea sweeping over her. We were fearful that the water would fill us through the cabin opening;

then the captain said that it would be better to close the cabin door, and that three men would do on deck. And that's how it was : the captain was steering and I was standing by him; the third men was for'ard of the mainmast. A particularly bad spell came when we were just between the two points at the harbour's mouth. A sea as big as a hill broke right over her and out over the cap of the prow, and with that the captain lost his grip and was knocked down. It was the will of God that I myself held on; if I hadn't we would have been in a bad way. I immediately took the captain's place; the boat shook herself free of the sea's grip, and before the second sea could strike her we had run into calm water.'

'Ye were lucky to escape,' said one of the neighbours who was in the house at the time.

'We were, but it was God's will that we were not to go.'

'And isn't it down to Church Strand ye went at that time?' I enquired.

'Yes, straightaway,' he said.

'Ye couldn't be in a better place; ye were in a harbour within harbours.'

'But when the gale was spent,' said Tomás, 'and when I gazed at the sky in the morning, and saw the bright happy harbour all about us, what went through my mind that very moment but the impulse to put the following words together in praise of God's mercy :

> I stand in awe before storm and waves,
> And the roar of the wind high in the sky,
> The jet black clouds and the brutal thunder,
> And no gleam of light coming from the sun.

> 'Twas the King of the world Who made them all,
> Both storm and sea-surge and the wind so loud;
> But His glowing powers are far greater yet,
> For gentle calm comes when such is His will.

> The sun will be shining from morning to night,
> And the moon in beauty take her seat in the air,
> The stars will attend and watch over each land :
> All praise to You for ever, O King of the Saints.

CHAPTER SEVEN

The smuggler on the coast; our hand in the dog's mouth.

Some forty years ago a vessel from Holland used to travel along this coast selling tobacco and brandy to the fishermen.[1] The captain, who was known as 'Lord John', couldn't come any closer to the land than three miles, for it would be against the law. No matter how the wind blew he had to put up with seas of all kinds, for the cutter was for ever on the watch, and if he came within the limit he would be arrested at once. But he was not obliged to move in close for the position in which he lay could always be discovered by us. The goods he had for sale were cheap : he used to ask for a shilling a pound for his tobacco which was made up in fine, sweet-flavoured 'cakes', each a half-pound in weight. Twenty-two pounds weight of that sort of tobacco was contained in a box for which the asking price was £1. The brandy was in jars holding a quart each, and the cost was two shillings for each jar.

Although he used to bring the full of his boat with him he wasn't long selling it among the fishermen here. He used to arrive here in the beginning of the season, and when he had sold the last of his cargo he used to leave for home.

That was the time that it was easy for a man to fill his pipe, whatever he would do now, a time when you could get a year's supply of tobacco for ten shillings. I suppose that day will never come again : it certainly didn't since then.

On a particular Friday evening which was exceedingly fine, when the boats were on the point of lowering sail and shooting, our captain said : 'There's the smuggler out there.' 'So he is,' we answered.

'I don't know lads,' said he, 'but we could do with buying some tobacco for fear he would soon have the last of it sold. It would come in very handy for us to get it now : it will be Saturday tomorrow and we needn't go into any harbour but straight home.' Naturally all we wanted was the wind of the word.

'Beckon him over to the boat,' said he. We didn't delay in giving the signal. One of the crew put an old bag on the point of an oar and the seller of wool understood the buyer of wool. We didn't have to wait long for the smuggler's punt to come alongside us. Every pair of the crew bought a box of tobacco between them, that is three and a half boxes in all—for the eighth member of the crew didn't smoke a pipe and only bought a pound of the outer skin : he used to put a plug of it in his mouth to chew because it was sweet tasting. Then we bought a quart bottle of brandy a man at two shillings a bottle, that is a total of twelve shillings worth of tobacco and spirits each.

We shot our nets that night and had a catch of two hundred mackerel. But we would have been better off not to get them for, instead of going home to Cape Clear—as we were saying on the previous night—we were obliged to go to the market with our fish. When we were under way in the morning all but two of the crew turned in. It happened that it was the captain and myself that remain on deck. That morning there was rain and a light fog, but still the sea was fine and calm, and we had a fair wind in making for the harbour. It was the captain who was steering the boat.

'By the Lord,' I said to him, 'it would be a good thing to have a hot drop to warm ourselves.'

'Perhaps that would be just right.' he said, I brought my bottle from the cabin, and a cup along with it and poured out a fair measure from it for my companion, and he drank it. I also had one.

'Good health to you,' he said, 'we are lucky to have this drop in the morning. But you had better stow all the stuff away in some place where it won't be seen for what the eye can't see won't worry it.'

'Where should I put them?' I replied.

'Pull up five or six nets from below and put the tobacco and brandy down near the bulwark and then cover them with the nets.'

I did as he said, except that I held on to my own bottle and didn't put it there at all.

'I don't know a thing about that man with the pound of tobacco, what about him?' I asked.

'I suppose he'll put it in his pocket,' said the captain.

I lowered the hatch again so that no one would think that we had anything like that stuff on board.

Once more I took the cork out of my bottle: 'We'll drink another small drop,' said I, 'and then I'll put it in a safe place until some other day.' We drank. I brought up an empty bottle in which there had been whiskey before hand for there was a label on its side. I emptied the brandy into it and threw the jar overboard. I put the other one ahide in the press.

By that time we were very close to the harbour. We hauled down the sails and anchored. There was a big fleet of boats at anchor all about the harbour, and I know that we dropped anchor on the northern edge of those, that is as far as we could go from the Custom Officers' station. We then ate our breakfast at our ease.

'I'll go ashore now,' said the captain, 'and get what money is coming to us after the week'—for it was on Saturday that the buyers used to pay the money—'and I'll be back on board as quickly as I'm ready, and we'll go home.' The punt was launched, and one of the crew headed for land.

The day didn't turn out as fine as we thought. It blew exceedingly hard from the south-west and we began to say among ourselves that this would be our berth for the night; and as ill-luck would have it that was where we stayed too—and for a whole week from that day.

There was one of the crew who was rather advanced in years, and it is usual that old people are more fretful about things than the young. So when the punt came back about two o'clock he said to the captain 'Well, my good friend, I would think that there is no sense staying here tonight with those goods on board, for we know that our hand is in the dog's mouth.'

'I know that well,' said the captain, 'but it's appallingly wet and threatening to blow, and I'm afraid that—if we sailed— we wouldn't be alive in the morning; it isn't a safe thing to be poking about and feeling one's way in the dark of a moonless night, and especially in such a dangerously narrow passage as the mouth of Trakieran with the wind blowing straight out the jowl of the harbour against us. It's as well for us to set our hearts at ease and remain here until morning.'

It wasn't long afterwards that we saw the Officers' boat

heading towards us from the south, with six men rowing and the Chief Officer in his military uniform and trappings steering her. One would think, however, from their course that they were making for some other point. But when they fetched up in line with our boat, they turned towards us and were aboard and in our midst in the twinkling of an eye. We became downcast and depressed for we knew that we had no way out. If only we had left, as the old fellow suggested a while back, there would be no fear of us; but it is after every action that a mistake is recognised too late, and we had certainly made a blunder.

The Chief Officer who had all the badges on his clothes enquired if we had anything on board on which we hadn't paid duty. Quite naturally we told him we hadn't. 'I'll have to search the boat,' he said. It was no use saying anything against him : the law was on his side, and so he was told that he could do that. He ordered his men to search the boat. Some of them went into the cabin, and more below deck for'ard. They didn't leave a hole or corner without rummaging there; even the old makeshift 'shakedowns' we had for beds were turned over.

To put the tin lid on it[2] one of them came across a slab of tobacco under the corner of a bed, whatever misfortune was on the person who owned it that he didn't put it in his pocket. When they got the first hint at all of such stuff, that sent them searching madly. 'I know that ye are not relying on that much tobacco,' said the Chief Officer, 'and if I don't find the rest I'll take the boat in to the quay, and I won't leave as much as a pound of ballast on board that I won't take out of her in order to locate it—take the hatch off the nets!' That last was a command to one of his men who carried it out. 'Lay hold of the end of those nets and haul them up,' he continued. That was the moment we became really scared for we knew only too well that they would find the hiding place in a short while. They found it—after five minutes. They put all that was in the cache on board their own boat. Then two of the crew remained on board our boat with us, and the rest of them went ashore with the contraband stuff. We were just the same as prisoners; there was only one thing left to say : 'Patience is best in a situation for which there is no remedy.'

The two officers who remained with us kept pacing up and

down the deck for eight hours, until two of their comrades came to take their places—and they then went ashore. They went on coming and going like that, two after two, day and night. When Sunday came around one morning, ambasa! weren't all of us, except for the captain, allowed to go to Mass; he was kept prisoner as a guarantee. We returned on board as speedily as we were able to. We didn't have a hard time for the King's men were taking care of us : our food was the concern of the foreigners and our beds were Irish and our own.

On Monday evening we saw the boat coming as was usual. We thought that it was for the purpose of changing the men; but no. Every single man of us was ordered to go aboard the boat. We did so, and they brought us ashore at the Custom's Station. We didn't know what they planned to do with us or where we were going. It was after they brought us ashore they told us where we were heading for.

They had a horse and coach harnessed outside the station. One of the officers got into the coach and called the captain of our boat to join him : 'I'll give you a lift,' he said. The second officer came towards us and ordered us to walk along with him.

'And where are we going now?' said I to him.

'We are bringing you all before the Justice,' he replied. 'It is four long miles to Lough Hyne if you know where it is.'

'I don't,' I answered, 'I was never there at any rate.'

We set off on the road, but because we had no experience of a long walk we thought that we would never get the journey over. The officer was gossiping and telling us stories, and that shortened the road greatly for us. When we reached the Justice's house the man with the horse and coach had got there long before us although he didn't go in until we were all gathered together.

We were led to the hall door; and indeed it was no excuse for a hall. Such animal skins were spread on the floor that you would scruple to walk on them with the sort of boots we wore, covered as they were with the scales of fish. But we were as good as we could be : 'You can't get wool from a goat' as the proverb puts it.

Next we were brought into a fine, big spacious room, and I

couldn't begin to describe the ornaments that were there. A big heavily-built, middle-aged man was lying back in a fine soft chair, with his back against a support, his shins warmed by a blazing red fire, and he was smoking a pipe. He had a fine, soft, civil look that hadn't a trace of bad temper or ferocity in it, and when he looked at us there was a flicker of laughter on his lips.

'What have these men done out of the way that you brought them before me?' he asked the officer.

The officer told him in full detail what the charge against us was, and how we had broken the law of the kingdom. When the man seated in the chair heard that much he reflected for five minutes before he uttered a word. He shook his head and looked at each man of us in turn.

'That charge against these men is too serious for me to settle on my own,' he said, 'and I won't take it on myself to do so. But let them appear before the bench in the Skibbereen Court House a week from next Wednesday.'

Out the door with us again to shorten the road back as best we could. When I looked about me after leaving the house I remarked to one of my companions : 'Hasn't that man inside a snug next for himself!'

'It's probably the same story with all of his sort in Ireland,' said he.

We were trudging along, sad and weary—for we were aware all the time of our being in a fix, and without a notion when we would get relief from our distress. We had travelled no more than three perches of the road when the horse and the pair in the coach disappeared from our sight. When we had walked about half the way back the officer asked us if we were hungry. We told him we weren't. 'Well,' said he, 'if anyone needs a bite I have bread and meat with me in a little parcel.'

'Thank you,' I said to him, ' 'twas a nice thought of yours; but if you have any drop in the bottle we'll drink it.' What did he do but laugh.

The two officers we had left behind us watching the boat were still there. Those two went ashore, and only one man was sent to keep an eye on us for that night.

We boiled the kettle for we needed some bit of supper after

all our travelling about. 'It's just the right time for us to be aboard,' I said, 'because it is nasty enough on deck, and if it lasts like that that poor "angishore"3 up there tramping the deck won't last the night.'

'I wonder if he were called down would he come?' said the captain.

I called up to him : 'It would be better for you to come below out of the rough weather and have a cup of tea to warm yourself. You're welcome if you come.'

All he wanted was half an excuse. He came down and the very first thing he did was to throw his bag of weapons on the seat beside him. I asked him was there anything dangerous in the bag. 'There's a pistol in it, but the safety-catch is on it,' he said as he opened the bag at the same time to show us all that was in it.

'Is that pistol loaded,' I asked.

'Yes,' he said, 'but I assure you that there's no danger in it.'

He took out a whistle too and the captain asked him what he wanted that for. 'Well,' he said, 'to blow it if I was in a fix so that help could come to me.'

He then showed us another item which we thought very odd, and he was asked what it was for. 'That is used at night,' he said. 'I am here on my own among eight of you, for example. Ye could throw me overboard, but if I got an opportunity to light this, the man on watch ashore would see the flash of light, and with the tap of a drum help would be at hand for me.' He looked from one to another of us. 'But I don't think I'll have any necessity to use these things as long as I am with ye.'

'Musha, did you ever drink a drop of the smuggler's brandy?' I asked him.

'I didn't,' he answered.

'Indeed,' said I, 'You won't be so because I'll give you a glass of it now,' as I pulled my bottle towards me; for it was full to the brim just as when I poured it in : the officers didn't take it away with them at all; they thought it was whiskey when the label was on it. I uncorked it, poured out a *taoscán* and handed it to him. 'Throw that back,' I said. He did so and thanked me. I handed a drop round to the others. 'By God,' I said, ' 'tis as

47

well for me not to put it away; since it was left with us, let us finish it.' We weren't long putting paid to it.

You never met such a fine fellow for spinning yarns as the officer when the drink softened him, and he told us what they used to do when he was on a frigate in the British Navy; how there were no smugglers in the world to equal them. 'But,' said he, 'we would pay dearly for it if we were caught.'

That is the way we spent the week until Friday evening. We lodged a complaint saying that it was a terrible way for us to be —idle until the day of the court without earning a penny. The Chief Officer sent a report to the Custom House and a reply came which set us free on our getting sureties, that is two people to go bail for us for £50 each.

We weren't long waiting before we found two men who went surety for us. The time was our own again and we went fishing, hoping to earn something that would clear the expenses ahead of us. Three nights fishing we had before the day for the Court, that is Wednesday. When we reached the harbour that morning, we went ashore and the train brought us to Skibbereen.

We couldn't have been more surprised at the sky's falling on the earth than when we heard the news on reaching the town, 'that no court would sit today because the Chairman of the Justices was dead and the funeral was to take place that very day.' A few hours after that a report arrived that the funeral was entering the town. And it certainly was a huge one : I'm sure that it stretched over two miles. We ourselves joined the mourners from that point as far as the Railway Station, for it was on a special train he was brought for burial in his native place. We were told that no court would sit for a fortnight from that day—as a sort of 'month's mind', or tribute to the person who was being buried.

As usual we went fishing again. When the fortnight was up, instead of remaining till the day our respite was over we went to the town on the previous evening. On the advice of good authorities we decided to hire an attorney to plead in our case, and went to his office where he wrote out a statement from us in accordance with what we told him; and, indeed, it would be hard to find a man who was more skilled than he was in legal matters. 'Things will go well for us,' he said, 'unless the other side has lawyers tomorrow.'

Lucky enough they hadn't.

The Court was to sit at twelve o'clock the following day. We waited anxiously for the time. When we entered the Court House the justices were already above in their seats. It was a bench of Protestants without as much as a single Catholic amongst them. We noticed that it was the Lough Hyne man who was Chairman.

Our case was put to the bench of judges. When they realised that an attorney was working for us they didn't like it, for they had no one to oppose him. And from their point of view the bad consequence was that the officers and the Custom House man were persuaded that black was white so that the case that day didn't last longer than an hour. The justices threw out the charge against us, without any costs falling on us either on that occasion. When the man from the Custom House realised that we had got off as softly as that he was furious. He addressed the justices and said : 'I'll summon these men again and I'll have the case called a fortnight from today, and I assure you that we will be in better order on that day. The fishermen were too clever for us today, but we can't allow people to break the law of the kingdom when it pleases them.'

It was true for him : the case was re-entered. We came home and said to one another that we should forget about what had happened, and face up to what lay before us : the Court once more.

CHAPTER EIGHT

The summons served again. — The second day in Court.
— 'A word in the court ...' — How the matter ended.

We bade goodbye to Baltimore that evening and vowed that
we wouldn't be seen there again until the fishing season was over
because there was only a fortnight of it left by that time.

We fished that fortnight without entering any harbour,
because we knew that the danger was still hanging over all our
heads—that is the threat of the summonses. The plan we had
to adopt was to shoot our nets close to a particular boat and put
our catch aboard it every morning; the owner used to sell it in
the fish-market along with his own catch.

Because we weren't entering harbour every day we were short
of food by the end of a week, and we said to one another that
no place was handier and less risky to get food in than Schull.
We anchored in Long Island channel where we couldn't be seen
from the village nor from the Custom's Station; for, quite
naturally, they always passed on the warning word to each
other. We launched the punt and the captain told me and
another one of the lads to go ashore and bring back some food
and water with us. 'And,' said he, 'don't ye make any delay
either, but as little as ye can, and let ye have only the briefest
gossiping with anyone ye meet.'

We set out, and had a mile to row from the time we left the
boat until we landed on the pier. What we had to do we did
with all speed and haste; but, to tell the truth, we had a pint
each to drink despite our hurry.

'By the Lord,' said I, 'the welt of my boot is torn; I'll have to
go to the shoemaker's and get a few stitches in it as my stocking
is wet every night because of it.'

In we went together. There were three shoemakers working
there. I took off my boot and gave it to one of them : 'Sew that
welt, and don't be long with it for I'm in a hurry.'

When he took the boot in his hand he said : 'Stand inside
away from the line of the door,' for he knew us quite well.
'Have ye been served with the second summons?'

'Not yet,' I answered.

50

'I'm afraid that ye won't be long so,' said he.

'Ye won't be,' said the local officer's son, who happened to be present during the conversation, 'for my father has the summonses for to give them to ye, and he'll be in Cape Clear any day from this out to serve ye with them. And my advice to ye is to leave the village as quickly as your legs will carry ye.'

We did as he counselled. When we reached the boat the captain asked us if we had any fresh news from the shore.

'Yes,' I answered, 'they are making no delay in coming after us.'

'How do you know that?' said the captain.

'I know well,' I said, 'that the officer in Schull has the summonses inside there, and we don't know the day that he'll be in our midst in Cape Clear to hand them to us.'

'Who was telling ye that?' he asked.

'Oh Musha, the officer's son whom we heard saying that they had been sent to his father; and he told us that he will be in Cape Clear tomorrow or the day after to serve us.'

'Wasn't it decent of him to give ye that much information?' said the captain.

' 'Tis from himself entirely the malice would come,' said the captain, 'for, to tell you the straight truth, he couldn't be different and take after his father at the same time. Bring the punt aboard, haul the anchor, and hoist the sail. We'll fish for the night as it will be a fine calm one.'

We did so, and spent the night fishing, and we didn't catch as much as would be worth sending to the market. We put in to Trakieran that morning : that was Saturday morning. We put our nets ashore and so that was the end of the mackerel fishing season for us that summer. We brought the boat into the dock and moored it. In the evening everyone headed for his own home for the first time in a fortnight. We would have one night in peace and at our ease at any rate.

All was well until the evening of the following day : about two o'clock we saw the officers' boat crossing the bay making for Trakieran. If so we scattered towards the hill, and you can take my word for it that it would be a hopeless job for them to be trying to find us in Cape Clear if we didn't want to be found. The upshot of that day's work was that nobody was served a summons except for the captain, because he didn't leave his house : he considered that he would be caught sooner or later. The officer was obliged to go back home and bring the balance of his papers with him. Meantime we were on the look out, like a cat watching a mouse : as quickly as we saw the officers' boat on its way back off with all of us home again.

A half-an-hour afterwards isn't it I was surprised when a messenger came from the priest looking for me.

'What does the priest want me for?' I asked.

'I don't know,' he said, 'but he ordered you to come to his house, and every one else for whom the officer had a summons today'.

We all gathered at the priest's house that evening.

'Well men,' said the priest to us, 'my counsel to you is that you go in the morning looking for the summonses, because I consider that the affair will look better if you all go together, for fear that the burden might lie too heavily on one man alone. Accept my advice and do what I am saying to you.' We promised him that we would.

As soon as we saw the first bright eye of the dawn we went off together and made for Schull, and straight for the house of the officer. There was no one in the kitchen apart from himself and his wife, and he was amazed when he saw us.

His wife looked at us and started to laugh. 'It's often I heard,' she said, 'that a person cuts a little stick in the wood in order to beat and hurt himself, and that's exactly the way it is with ye today.[1] And I'd think, boys, that it was very foolish of ye to come all the way from Cape Clear today looking for those "papers".'

'Perhaps it was the best thing ever for them to come,' said the officer. 'I'm very thankful to ye, and I hope that things will be easier on ye than ye expect. I'll see ye again the day of the court.'

We left him and were back home early in the evening, each of us having his own 'white horse' in his pocket.[2] That much was done; but the trouble was that we had no time to cool our heels for we must be on the road again tomorrow. We had to be in the town the night beforehand in order to get the special instruction of the attorney about the one matter of importance, that is—what was best for us to do.

'I'm afraid,' he said, 'that as far as tomorrow's case goes we are in trouble for those officers will have crown lawyers tomorrow to oppose you. I'll do my best, however.'

We went into a pub to have a drink. We were well-known in the town and everyone knew what brought us there. Everyone was sympathising with us and telling us that a man would be in the chief justice's chair the following day who wouldn't let us off lightly 'for,' they said, 'he seldom comes to Skibbereen—only if there's a serious case to be settled just as yours is.'

Four of us went off together to arrange for lodgings in a house where we usually stayed any night we would be in town. The chairman tomorrow was the sole talk of the man of that house exactly like everyone else. He told us that it was his usual custom to impose a prison-sentence instead of a fine on people. We were shocked and dismayed, just as if a stone struck us in a bush where we were hiding, when we heard that news.

The same four of us left to go for a short stroll around the town for we thought it too early in the evening to remain indoors. While we were walking we met the other four members of the crew.

'Where are ye staying tonight?' I enquired.

'In North Street,' they replied.

'We are lodging in North Street also,' I said, 'and that is the place where we are closest to the Court House for tomorrow.'

When it was getting late the four of us returned to the lodging house. When we entered I spoke up and said : 'Let ye sit down on the "form" there and I'll stand each of you a half-one even if the devil were to enter the closed door.'

While filling out the drink the man of the house asked us if we had heard the latest news. We told him we hadn't and that we hoped to God it was good.

'It's like this,' he said, 'the justice who was to be in the chair won't be there at all tomorrow.'

'Why won't he be there?' I asked.

'I don't know,' he said, 'but a telegram came to the town a while ago saying that he fell from his horse and that he is in hospital with the ball of his hip-joint out of its socket.'

53

While he was saying that a bit of a gentleman came in the door; a cane in his fist, a long-tailed coat on him, and garters around the calves of his legs. He stood against the counter and asked the man inside to fill out a glass of whiskey for him.

The man of the house spoke in Irish to us and said : 'Here is one of the justices who will be on the bench tomorrow, and if you could make his acquaintance it wouldn't do ye any harm.'

'Would you have another drop of that, please?' I said as soon as I saw his empty glass. He looked at me in bewilderment because he didn't understand me; but the man of the house told him in English that I was offering him a drink. He accepted the offer gratefully. He took glass after glass until he had drunk a fair lot. At this point the woman of the house said : 'Your supper is ready; go into that room there.' The man nearest to me on the 'form' had a good smattering of English and I whispered to him that it would be as well to ask the frock-coated man would he like to go in and have a cup of tea along with us. He joined us and sat at the table with us and proved to be a very civil person indeed.

'Diarmuid,' said I, 'ask him does he know who will be in the chair on the bench tomorrow.' He did so.

'The man from Lough Hyne,' was his answer. 'And was it court business that brought ye to town tonight?'

Diarmuid said that it was, and he told him the whole story, word for word, from beginning to end.

'I will be one of those on the bench tomorrow,' he said, 'and indeed, poor men, I won't do you any harm, but good, instead, if I can. Goodbye now; I'll see you tomorrow and I trust the affair won't be as hard and troublesome as you anticipate,' and so he went out the door from us.

'Musha,' said I, 'I wonder did our comrades hear anything about the man with the broken leg? I'll run out and tell them about it. It would be a great easing of mind for them, unless they have already found out about it.'

It wasn't far distant : only up a few doors. They had heard nothing about it up to then.

In the morning we had a little breakfast before we went out. 'The train isn't in yet,' said I, 'let us go as far as the station.'

Before we reached the place the train was in, and the people

54

coming against us. We recognised the Baltimore officer among them with another one of them. While he was passing us he didn't actually salute us but instead he glanced at us with a sly slanting motion of his head.

'It doesn't look as if he is pleased with us,' I said.

We hadn't gone much farther when we met the officer from Schull. But he didn't have a cross or cranky look; instead he saluted us civilly, and asked us how we were since he saw us last.

'We have our health, thanks be to God,' we said.

He took his watch out of his pocket. 'We have lashings of time left yet,' he said. 'Come on in here and I'll stand ye a drink for I suppose it won't be long till it will be low water in your pockets.'

'It's that way already,' we remarked, 'and your offer is just at the right time for us.'

In we went and everyone took the drink he liked.

'Well,' said the Schull officer, 'whatever I am able to do I'll do. I could charge you with £5 expenses for that day I went to Cape Clear to serve the summonses; but I'll suffer the loss of that myself because I'm afraid that ye'll have enough to contend with in the way of costs without taking that into account.'

'Long life to you and may your prosperity last,' we said to him together.

'Boys,' said I after he went, 'isn't that a great difference between two men.'

'There is no comparison,' one of them said in answering me, 'in putting that fine easy-going man just gone on a level with the man who wouldn't salute a person on the road.'

It wasn't long before we reached the Court House. We went in, and you could hardly make your way through the people there : the place was packed from the back to the door. All the justices were in their places. There were three other strangers there that we hadn't seen at all at the first trial : those were the lawyers the other side had on this occasion; for they had bought wisdom dearly from their previous experience and, 'signs on', they weren't caught napping this time.

We sat near our own attorney for he wanted to put a question to us, now and then, as it suited him.

Our case was the first one called that day. The charge against us was read out from the bench. Our attorney then spoke in our defence as well as he was able to. But his argument didn't get very far for it got short shift from those men who were able to match him in debate, and dispute his pleading, that is the crown lawyers. The two sides almost got to the point of spitting at one another about points of law, our own attorney opening every gap and those closing them. They were at it like that for four solid hours; so that clearly our own man didn't leave a stone unturned in defending us. But the upshot was that they got the better of him in the long run. There was a gauger there from the Custom House who had some of the seized goods on the bench, and was telling the court what duties applied to them. He took a hunk of the tobacco out of his pocket and handed it to one of the justices, then he gave him a half-pint of the spirits. They all scrutinised them closely handing them from one to the other; but when the bottle reached our man who had been in the lodging-house pub talking to us the previous night, he put it to his lips and I promise you that he took a fine gulp of it. 'Ah,' said he, 'that's a grand drink!' The other justices looked at one another with astonishment.

Then the Chairman of the Justices read out the Act and said that each one of us was being fined £13 or alternatively fourteen days in Cork Prison.

No sooner had the Chairman said that much then two constables who had been on duty at the door all day pounced on us, and bundled us together into a kind of cell around the edge of which high iron spikes were fixed. But they had done this far too quickly for they hadn't received the permission of the bench of justices. In fact while they were doing it the justices were only occupied with filling out the warrants to make prisoners of us. Our man who took the swig out of the bottle a while ago spoke : 'I won't put my name today to any warrant sentencing these men!' just as he was going down from the bench and going out a backdoor there.

At the same time our attorney took a letter out of his pocket, and handed it to the Chairman. When he had read it he gave it to the man nearest to him, and so on. They spent a spell then whispering among themselves. It wasn't long until the Chairman spoke out and said : 'I am going to give these men one more chance as it was the first act they ever did out of the way and their first time ever in court—and also, since I have a good report of their reputation for honesty and their integrity of character. Go home now and get a recommendation in writing from your priest. Sign all your names to it and send it to the Viceroy in Dublin, and let whatever he will say be the ultimate decision of the law.'

We came home with new heart in us and on the same evening went to the priest's house. He did the writing for us and we put our names to it. The priest sent it off for us. 'The reply,' he said, 'will probably come to me and we should have it in a week's time.'

Instead of news coming to the priest, it was to the Chairman of the Justices it came, leaving it to him to make whatever decision he wished. He sent us a message ordering us to pay a fine of ten shillings a man, and saying that he couldn't be easier on us.

What was responsible for our getting out of the case so lightly was the letter from the parish priest that was handed in to the bench of Justices on the day of the trial. I am positive that there wasn't another man of his kind in the county in his day, not one whose recommendation would be trusted like his. But for that we were properly done for. It has always been said and it is a true saying that 'a word in the court is better than a pound in the purse.'

I thought that I would never again hear any reference to that affair; but that wasn't so. On a windy evening at sea, fifteen years afterwards, we ran for shelter to Crookhaven. We were spiller-fishing that same week and had a couple of 'scrawls'3 of baited trawl-lines at work; and we were saying that if the following morning was suitable for it that we would get another day's fishing out of it before going home. We dropped anchor in Crookhaven at twilight.

Every man used to bring his own food supplies with him when it was time for catching 'green-fish', that is fish like hake which were cured.

'I'd better go ashore to get some bread,' remarked one of the

57

crew. Another said that he hadn't any tobacco. The punt was launched, and five of the crew boarded her. 'Whoever remains on board,' said the captain, 'let him have the kettle boiled when we are back because we won't make any delay.'

Off they went. Nobody remained on board apart from myself and a young boy. The kettle was boiled, and we made the tea and were having a cup each when we heard a boat coming alongside.

'By the Lord, Donnacha,' I said, 'they certainly didn't make any delay ashore.'

'They couldn't be back yet,' he said, 'and I'll bet you that she is the Custom Officer's boat'—for, whatever harbour a boat entered the Officer's duty was to board her and naturally their likes were in every harbour around the coast.

My young companion was right : the last word was hardly out of his mouth when the Officer jumped on board. He looked down into the cabin and asked if the captain was on board. It was I who answered him and I told him that he wasn't but that he would be shortly. 'Come on down,' said I to him, 'and sit down with us for a while; they'll be here before long.' As soon as I clapped eyes on him I guessed who he was.

He came down and seated himself. I noticed that he was examining me closely and at last, he blurted out as if a blister of curiosity in him had burst :

'I saw you somewhere before.'

'Where would you see me?' I said.

'I did see you,' he went on; 'you were one of the crew of that boat we found the tobacco and spirits in fifteen years ago in Baltimore.'

I hesitated for a couple of minutes :

'You are right there,' I said; 'I was. And the very moment I saw your face I recognised you too. Aren't you the man who found the first bit of tobacco we had that day?'

'I am,' he replied.

'And now,' I went on, 'that that affair is over and past long ago I am sure that ye wouldn't have made for our boat, purposely above all the other boats in the harbour that evening, unless ye got a tip-off from someone who was spying on us.'

'Of course we did,' he admitted.

'May he not get the reward for his labour!' I said, 'whatever person told you. I suppose that he wouldn't have told only that he got the bait of some bribe as a result.'

He didn't say a word about that to me.

'Indeed,' said I to him, 'that day taught me and everyone who was in the one company with me—a new lesson which we remembered : for it has been said that "The child who is burned is afraid".'

CHAPTER NINE

A stranger learns about the lore of the Island.

I was cutting a fistful of ferns with a scythe this time three years ago in the month of September on a fine sunny day, and I was working close to the road. I had my head bent while I was sharpening my scythe. I had no thought that anyone was next or near me when a man spoke behind me, from out on the road.

'God bless the work,' said he.

I raised my head and looked at him.

'Amen, Lord, and the same to you too!'

I noted that he was a visitor whom I had never seen before then.

'What use will you make of those ferns?' he enquired.

'Well it's for the fire when it will be withered.' He looked at me with surprise:

'I never heard before that a fire was made out of ferns.'

'When nothing can be found in its place,' I said, 'a fire is made of it.'

'And isn't there any turf-bank in the Island,' he asked.

'There isn't, musha, nor a single sod of turf. It's easy to see that you don't know anything about the Island when you put that question to me.'

'I don't,' he said; 'I am making my first visit to the Island today.'

'Where are you from, please?' I said.

'I'm from Dublin. I landed about an hour ago from the mail-boat that came from Baltimore, and I would like to stay for a week with somebody who would tell me the story of the Island. Do you know anyone about the place who would give me lodgings for a week?'

I hesitated for a while and then said that I would try to do it myself.

'Thank you,' said he, 'I'm very grateful to you.'

He came along with me to the house. A fine, easy-going chatty man he was, and indeed there was no sign that he was wanting

60

in his knowledge of Irish. We were yarning until the supper was ready.

'I don't consider anything on this Island strange or surprising,' I said to him.

'It isn't so for me,' he commented; 'everything I have seen so far is fascinating and when you will tell me the whole story it will surely be more interesting. For, to tell you the truth, there are hundreds of thousands of my sort throughout Ireland.'

All that amazed me when I heard it, but I suppose that wasn't right for me; for, if I and my like were to go into the cities in Ireland they would seem as strange to us as Cape Clear did to him.

I'll tell you all about the gossip and storytelling of every kind that we had during the week he spent in my company.

When we had eaten our supper we had an hour's chat until bedtime came.

'I thought,' he said, 'that the Island wasn't half a big as it is.'

'Ambasa,' said I, 'it is much larger than one would ever conceive.'

'Could you tell me the length and breadth of the Island?'

'I could,' I said; 'it is three miles long from Lickeen in the east to Ligaunach in the west, and two miles broad from Carriglure[1] in the south to the Poor Woman's Cabin on Carriganayshk on the north side of the Island.'

'I will have to see those places you've named. Will you go along with me tomorrow and show them to me?'

'Fair enough,' I said. 'We'll go as far as Lickeen in the eastern end first, and then we'll make our way westwards from there.'

We were ready to move off about nine o'clock in the morning, and when we went out of the house he looked about him and like anyone in a strange place he asked me : 'Where will we go now?'

'We'll take a short-cut to Lickeen.'

I had my reasons for saying that for there were 'gallawns' or pillar-stones, on the way which I wanted to show him. When we got as far as them we stopped, and he asked me if I had ever heard any story or tradition connected with those three 'gallawns'.[2]

61

I told him I had : 'Do you see that "gallawn" with the hole right through it? It is often I heard that in the time of the pagans long ago before the faith was in Ireland, they used to be married at that "gallawn"—that is, the pair to be married would hold one another's hands through that hole. The king of the pagans used to be present and so they were married in his presence. Another account I heard of the "gallawns" says that they were three warriors who were under a magical spell.'

We left them there and went in the direction of Lickeen. On our way past Coosanvaud which is west of Lickeen he asked me if I had any story about that cove.

'I heard a wonderful story about it,' I said, 'and it was about a sea-pirate who was fleeing from a frigate in olden times. He made a run from the coast into the mouth of that cove, and when he put the headland between himself and the frigate she lost sight of him in such a way that her crew thought he was lost; they didn't follow him any farther. The pirate had a firkin of gold on board which he had taken from some ship he had sunk on the previous day.

' "Well now," said the pirate captain, "we'll put the gold ashore here."

'He himself and six of his men landed and carried the firkin with them. They made a hole in the ground in some place at the edge of the cove and buried the firkin there.

'The captain then asked : "Will any man remain to guard that?" There was a negro there and he said that he would stay to watch it. The poor fellow had no thought of any evil. He didn't realise what was afoot until the captain took a pistol out of his pocket and shot him.

' "Well now," he said to the rest of the crew, "throw him down into the hole with the gold and let him guard it !" They pitched him in and filled up the hole, and they are there together from that day to this.'

We travelled on until we went as far as Lickeen. When we reached it he asked what was to be seen there.

'Nothing at all,' I said; 'the only thing is that the length of the Island is measured from here. Let us go south from here across the fields as far as Coosadooglish, and then we'll have the main road under our feet.'

We were walking along together, and he glanced across the sound towards the east in the direction of Sherkin Island.

'Have you any names for those rocks I can see?' he asked as he pointed towards them.

'Yes,' I replied, 'that one closest to you is Gaiscanaun; the second one is Carrigvuar and the third one, the one nearest to the island yonder, is Carrignaburtaun.'

'I think,' he said, 'that I heard tell of Gaiscanaun some way or other, and did you yourself hear any story about it?'

'I heard this much. A man whose name was Finín Mac Gearailt lived in Cape Clear long ago. One day that he went to the mainland he met a man who put a question to him:

' "Finín Mac Gearailt when will a day of flood come without rain?"

'He answered and said :

A man with my name is no poet, and to singing I wasn't born :
But if on Gaiscanaun rock you were sitting high up until morn
When a flood will come without rain you would know well and
    true before dawn.'

My visitor burst our laughing. 'And how could that be?' he asked.

'Well,' I said, 'you can see a large part of that rock exposed because the tide is low. Later on the flood tide will cover it so that you wouldn't know that the like of it was there at all. If a horse were standing on it, not to mind a person, the tide would sweep him away—it rushes so fiercely over the rock.

'As to those other rocks I heard nothing interesting about them except that a Portuguese vessel was wrecked and lost in olden times on the southern side of Carrigvuar. From that day to this, that part of it has the name of the Rock of the Portuguese. The crew survived, and I heard that the captain said that the ship wouldn't be lost if he had a big anchor he left at home on board. Ever since there's a common saying here about anyone who forgets anything : "Ah, you left it at home as the Portuguese left the big anchor at home after him!" '

By that time we were plodding along south through Lacka Lochaleen.

'That is a pool,' I said, 'where they used to "pond" or steep flax long ago—although I don't recall seeing it. *Loch an Lín* (or, The Lake of the Flax) is its name.'[3]

'Do you ever remember seeing flax growing on the Island?' he asked.

'Just barely,' I said; 'but we'll have another discussion about that yet.'

By that time we were standing on the road at Coosadooglish which goes right through the length of the Island.

'Where will that road bring us?'

'To the lake in Ballyieragh,' I said, 'or to any other part of the Island we'd like to head for.'

Up the road we climbed until we got as far as Killyvroon. I told him that tradition had it that there was a pagan graveyard there long ago, and he halted in order to examine the place closely.

'I notice,' he said, 'that the graves can still be seen and even the very headstones.'

'Yes,' I remarked, 'but the place is all rough ground and a tangle of coarse grass now, and a stranger to the Island wouldn't pay any attention to it unless he heard talk about it. There's a well of pure spring water inside the ditch of that small potato patch alongside us. It is called Tubbernakille and it never ran dry.'

'I'll go in to look at that well,' he said. He did so and drank a sup of the water, remarking that it was cold and excellent to taste.

'Yes,' I said, 'in fact one of the best wells of spring water in Ireland is to be found in this Island. And now that we are talking about the best and most excellent things, did you ever hear tell of a man whose name was Conchúr Mac Eirevaun?'

'The whole world heard about him,' he said. 'Wasn't he one of the strongest men in the province of Munster? Where did he live?'

'We're not three perches from the house where he lived,' I answered him. 'There it is to the north!'

'And do you tell me that he lived in that house there?'

'I have always heard so.'

'I suppose there was no limit to his strength.'

'None,' I remarked, 'according to all that is said about him. I heard that he had a boat moored in Coosadooglish once and that it blew hard one night so that a storm rose. His father called him and woke him from his sleep. "Conchúr," he said, "the boat will be gone in the morning unless you do something about her." He got up at once and went to look after her, and but for the speed with which he got to her there wouldn't be trace or tidings of her before him. He hauled her towards him up on the rock, and then lifted her up on his back across his two shoulder-blades, and carried her home. He put her down there at the north end of the house, upside down. When he went in home his father asked him was the boat safe. "I'll go warrant for her until morning, at any rate," he replied, "whether it blows hard or not." "And what did you do with her and where is she?" asked the old man. "You'll see her in the morning," he said, and went back to sleep again.'

'When was that man alive?' said the visitor to me.

'I suppose it is more than two hundred years ago.'

'And do you know if there are any of his relatives on the Island today,' he went on.

'I imagine that if anyone traced his relationship to him that he is dead and buried now,' I said.

'Have you any name for that hill there to the south?' he enquired.

'That is Knockfoilandirk,' I said, 'and do you see that big high rock at the top of the hill? Well, that's Carrigeenanillir, and the old people of the place used to say that an eagle often rested on it, and that the rock got the name of the 'Little Rock of the Eagle' as a result of that.'

'Let us shorten the road again,' he said, and when we were walking once more he asked me if I had ever heard of any other gaisce or feat that Conchúr Mac Eirevaun had accomplished.

'I did' I said. 'I heard that he was standing one day on the quay in Cork and that he saw six men trying to drag some, heavy object out of the slob of the river. The task was besting them. Conchúr asked them what they were doing and they said that a ship's anchor was buried down there. "We'll have to give over," they said. "Hand me the end of that chain," said Conchúr. They did so and he caught a grip of it in his two fists. "Move back from it!" he ordered. The first jerk he gave it loosened it from its hold; with the second try he brought it up as far as the bottom of the quay wall, and from there he brought it up hand over hand on to the quay. I heard that it was five hundredweight. But of course those men never dreamed that he would ever be able to accomplish the feat at all and they simply wanted to have a bit of fun by making a butt of him. However, when they saw the anchor on the quay they shouted, "Shame on you! You have done us out of earning our pay!" What did he do then but catch hold of the anchor and throw it twice as far out as it had been before so that it was much more firmly stuck! "There now," he said as he left them, "go and earn your pay!" '4

We had arrived at the priest's garden by the time I finished my story about Mac Eirevaun.

'Let us stop a while,' said I, 'till I tell you about a priest named Father Laurence O'Mahony who was here in Cape Clear about a hundred and thirty years ago.'5

'I suppose you have a great number of yarns about him.'

'I have a fair number,' I said, 'and I heard some of his poetry too from my grandmother.'

'I suppose she saw him,' he said.

'She remembered his being there—What time is it now?'

'Two o'clock,' he answered.

'Well it's fully dinner-time and so it is high time for us to go home. After our dinner we'll take it easy and I'll tell you whatever I know about him.'

When we reached the house the dinner was ready for us. Afterwards we had a rest for a smoke of tobacco. When our bellies were well-filled and warmed, and we had had our smoke, he asked me to recite some of the poetry composed by the priest which I heard from my grandmother.

'Well,' I said, 'I heard her saying that he used to have a special boat to bring him smuggled supplies; but on one particular voyage she was longer in coming than she should be: in fact he had given her up for lost she was so long overdue. Anyway he composed an elegy for her like this:

I would greatly prefer to Cape Clear and Creeg,
And the City of Troy all free without rent,
Or a gold-hafted blade in my hand from the King,
To be capering on a stage with "Love of my Heart".

I have rheumatics in my hip and all down my legs,
And there's no nurture for my stomach in any sort of food,
But as a strange one I watch from each ditch on my way
As I'm waiting for a hail from "Love of my Heart".

When the moon is declining in the sky full of stars,
And all the people in the land seek their beds out for rest
I can't sleep a wink or scarce think of lying down
But must hearken for a call from "Love of my Heart".

'But one particular morning that he left his house, wasn't he surprised to see her sailing on a tack northwards from the mouth of Coosadooglish towards Gaiscanaun. He got new heart from the sight and made a further verse :

Nicely my darling steps out a Scots reel
And as lightly she dances the Isle of Man;
My heart beat as hard as a bettering wind
When she danced up and down in front of my eyes.[6]

'And here is another piece of poetry of his which he made about himself, pretending that someone else composed it :

I travelled through Ireland, Scotland and England,
And all over France and so onwards to Rome
where bishops and priests were as countless as churches
Yet I never met his match anywhere that I went.

He could read books in Latin and of course those in English,
And as well say the Mass and preach a fine sermon,
He was generous, cordial and kindly moreover,
And to his well-loaded table you were always right welcome.'

'I suppose,' said our visitor, 'that when there was that much there must be more in existence.'

67

'Yes, wisha, and twice as much more, if I could only remember them. My grandmother was heard to say that he used to come to their house on a visit often to have a gossip with her father—for they lived near him. She said that one day that he came by the road to see them that her mother had a habit out on a bush, airing in the sun, and that no one could conceive of a decoration that wasn't sewn in threads of every colour on to the habit. The priest took the habit up in his hands and kept looking at it for quite a while. It happened, at the time, that there was a pot of boiled tree-bark beside the ditch for cutching the sail of a boat. The priest walked over to the pot and threw the habit into it and stirred it with a stick; then he lifted it out and said : "It is all one colour now, Máire Mhór, for no ornament is in keeping with the clay." That's the treatment he gave the garment after all the trouble she gone to making it!

'Another thing I heard her saying about him was that her mother used to grind a bag of wheat with a hand-quern for him, because mills were not as plentiful at that time as they are now; and, by the way, those same querns can be seen today just as good as they were at that time, and still doing the same job.'

'I'll certainly have to see those,' he said, 'they are so ancient.'

'There's no need for you,' I said, 'there's a pair of them out there by the ditch.'

'Is there then?' and he got up from the chair and went out to look at them. 'Is that kind plentiful?'

'Yes, there wasn't a house in the Island without a pair of them, because it was with them they used to grind as much grain as they had in olden times. But I also heard that there was some sort of a mill here that was worked by water, but nobody has any knowledge of when it was there. But there is proof still that it existed for the quern-stone is there, and I'll show you the place in which it was before you leave the Island.'

'Do you make any use of these ones now?' he enquired.

'We do,' I answered. 'Don't you see that there's a wooden plug and spindle in them and that they are still in working order? We often prepare the makings of *ríobún* from meal ground by a quern.'[7]

'I never ate any *ríobún*,' he said.

68

'Indeed you won't be long so, for we'll harden a handful by toasting it tomorrow, and we'll grind it.'

The evening was well on by that time, and we had finished our day's business.

'Well, good man,' I said, 'we've been yarning and chatting since yesterday evening, would you please tell me your name?'

'I will,' he said, 'and you're welcome. Call me Aindréas or Aindí.'

'Very well. May you live long to bear it, my decent fellow.'

'I suppose,' he said, 'that it's as well for us all to have a rest until dawn. Tomorrow is another day.'

'Yes,' I agreed. 'When tomorrow comes it will bring its own allotted share of life with it.'

CHAPTER TEN

*The crooked sickle or the sea-wrack hook — The view
from the top of the hill — They are the jealous hands!
— The ríobún — Thatching and basketmaking.*

At ten o'clock in the morning we were ready for the road
again. When we stood outside the door he looked about him.

'I suppose that there's a grand view to be seen from the peak
of that hill?' he said.

'Yes,' I said, 'as fine as you would see in any place you
walked.'

'And what is it's name?' he asked.

'That is Quarantine Hill, the highest hill in the Island.'[1]

He saw an old rusty blade on the yard ditch and asked me
what I called it.

'It is called either a "scowdoor" or a "curawn caum",' I said,
'whichever you prefer. Didn't you ever see the like of it?'

'Indeed I didn't,' he replied. 'What was it used for?'

'They were in use long ago to cut the *loke,* that is a special
kind of seaweed, in order to manure the potato gardens.'

'Do you remember that work being done?' he asked me.

'It must be the very oldest memory I have,' I answered.

'And how was the *loke* cut with the like of that?' he enquired.

'Well,' I said, 'when that was in proper order for work it had
a pole handle, that is a wooden haft, that was sixteen feet long;
and when there was a small tide and the *loke* wasn't exposed so
that it could be cut by the hand sickle, then they used to turn
to the "scowdoor" in order to cut the seaweed on the deep hidden
rocks that were never dry at any state of the tide. There were
four men in each boat attending to that work, two of them
working with "curawns", and the two others keeping the boat
steady over the *loke* rocks with the help of two oars.'

'Where were those implements made for them?'

'In the forge of course.'

'And was there a smith in Cape Clear at that time?'

'There wasn't,' I replied, 'neither I nor my father before me
remember any smith being in the Island, but I heard him saying
that a smith was living in this townland of Knockaunna-

70

maurnach, and that it would be in or about three hundred years since he was there. And I know myself where he lived because the wall of the forge can still be seen in a field of ours which we call the Forge Field.'

We went to see it, and he asked me if I knew the name of the smith.

'Liam Mac Taidhg's forge I have always heard said. There's another old relic over there,' I said, 'an old cutting machine.'

'What was that used for?'

'For crushing furze for cows long ago before machines were available for the job; and indeed the machine was a great comfort when compared with the cutter.'

Then he asked me how the furze was crushed with the cutter, and I told him I would tell him if he came along with me so that I could show him where and how the work was done. He did, and I showed him the trough. ' 'Tis many a back-load of french furze I myself crushed in that same trough, and that was the toilsome sweaty work. It was often I had to sharpen my cutter three times before I had my load of furze crushed. However, I can safely say to you that a basket of crushed furze was a fine supper for making a cow a good milker.'[2]

' 'Twas a wonderful trial of you to keep that old relic so long.'

'Why so man?' I said, 'only that somebody kept them they couldn't be seen or found today : they would have disappeared without any knowledge of their fate; and wouldn't you say now that that would be a great pity?'

'I would; and if everyone was as good as yourself at preserving such things, they would be found in plenty.'

' 'Tisn't that but this,' I said, 'the day is passing and our business isn't done.'

'You're right there,' he said, 'the distractions of the morning put all thought of the hill out of my head.'

We left home together, availing of every short-cut; and the state of the case was that Aindí had to be waiting for me because he had sinewy legs and my old bones were sluggish and weary. At long last we reached the top of the hill and truly there is no lie in saying that it was a fine, bright day of glowing, luminous sunlight.

He remained standing there for five minutes before he uttered a word. 'Well!' he then said, 'no matter where I have walked before, be it far on near, the grandest view that a sinner's eye could behold is to be seen from here at this time of day.'

'I will give you cause to say that in a moment,' said I. 'There before us is the broad coast to the south and the sea is as still as the ducks' pond, gloriously calm.'

'What is that headland in the east, as far as my eye can see, on which there are some white buildings?' he asked.

'That is the Galley Head lighthouse, if you ever heard tell of it. And those are the rocks called the Stags or Stacks on this side of it; and that other little island closer to us than them is Kedge Island where you can see the bed of Diarmuid and Gráinne.[3] Between that island and the mainland you can see three small rocks; they are the Three Steps that Diarmuid took to cross to the island with Gráinne on his back—when he was fleeing from Finn Mac Cumhaill.'

'What do you call that long point at the eastern end of this Island?'

'That is Cooslahan Point, and there is Pouladirk on this side of it—that long narrow cove you can see cutting right into the land; and still further west are the promontories of Rourvuar and Rourveg, and that point nearest to us, and just below us, is called Bossnaraharsee.'

'Are those tilled potato fields that I see down there close to the rocks? Wasn't it far from the houses they were made whenever they were cultivated?'

'I heard that they were made before the Year of the Famine, for anywhere there was a sod of earth to be found at that time in any patch at all between rocks the soil there was tilled; indeed potato gardens were made in spots where you would say—if you saw them—that it wouldn't be fitting for any living thing to go there except for some four-footed beast. There are many such ridges that were planted then that no spade was ever used on again, and they still look exactly as they were then because there was nothing in them to harvest.'

'There must have been a lot of people living in the Island at that time.'

'Yes, there was. I often heard that there were 1,200 people in

72

the Island before the Famine.[4] That was a great number of people living in such a small island, without their having much means except what they could win from the soil and the sea : and just as I told you a while ago, they had to till every single sod of the land in order to feed themselves. I heard that it was potatoes and barley that were planted in the Island then. That is the time that the potatoes were as plump and floury as the poet said :

> If we only set them in the middle of the Rock
> The smallest spud weighed at least a pound;
> Oro, and aren't the Horses a marvellous sight!

'They used to grind the grain with hand-querns and they had enough food of their own from one end of the year to the other until the Famine came. Hunger and fever fell on the Island and utter ruin seized the people, so that there is only about a third of that population here today. It shows all the signs too, for you couldn't go into any part of the Island where you wouldn't see the old ruins and walls of houses. There is a big change in the world today : there are fine, large houses throughout the Island in place of the thatched *bohauns* that were there then.'

'Isn't that a fine white lofty tower on the hill to the south west.'

'That is the lighthouse that was in Cape Clear before the light was transferred to the Fastnet Rock, and the name on that hill where the tower was built is Knockeenantowick. And just there below it you can see Foilneecahill, the highest cliff in the Island.'

'Have you any recollection of a light being there?'

'No,' I said, 'nor was there one for a good few years before my time. It is eighty-seven years since the light there was changed to the Fastnet Rock.'[5]

'And what about that old black ruin near it? Is that long built?'

'I heard old people saying that that old square tower was erected during the Napoleonic war.[6] That's Carriglure there in the south and, as I heard said, the reason it got that name was that a fleet of French boats used to fish round this coast long ago, and they were called 'lures' (*liúireanna*): each one had three masts and there were three lug sails on each mast. One of them was wrecked on that rock and ever since its name is Carriglure ... But see how absent-minded I've become that I didn't tell you that it is a hundred and thirteen years since the light in the lighthouse here was first lit.'

'Did you ever hear any explanation of the reason it was shifted from there?'

'I'll tell you why : it was too high up, and the fog used to fall on it too often and too quickly so that it couldn't be seen from the sea. There is Slieve Ard, the hill you can see furthest from you in the west! There are standing stones, called "The False Men", on that hill.'[7]

He was surprised to hear such a name for mossy grey stones.

'Ach ayeh, don't be a bit surprised at the name : there's more than that in the story. They were dressed like soldiers with a cap and red coat on every stone of them because, just as in the matter of the reference to the black tower a while ago, they were erected there in the time of the Napoleonic war to frighten the enemy when he saw them from the water.'

'Well, Conchúr, let no one talk,' he said, 'there's no limit to human ingenuity.'

'No, man; but that wouldn't go far in comparison with the ingenuity of our time for they are passing all bounds now. We were talking about the Fastnet Rock a while ago. When I was a child I used to hear old people saying that that rock was enchanted; that it used to travel east once a year on Mayday morning, in the guise of a sailing ship with three masts and full canvas, and head for the Stag Rocks; it used whisper to them and go back to its berth; that journey was completed before the sun rose. The name it was called at that time was "the Swan of the Jet-black Carn bereft of light in the dark". But since I made its acquaintance it is there without stirring and will remain so for ever.'[8]

'Are there any other sights to be seen in the western end of the Island?'

'There are,' I said, 'I often heard that a warrior of the Fianna of Ireland was buried there to the west on the top of a cliff called Foilyearmuda, that is Diarmuid's Cliff. And there's some solid proof that he was because the tombstone over him can still be seen. I'll tell you how I heard the *seanchaí* explaining the way it happened that Diarmuid came to Cape Clear.

'The Fianna were hunting one day and a boer's bristle pierced the palm of Diarmuid's hand while he was measuring it. The bristle poisoned his hand, and the pains got worse and worse as no cure could be found for it. Finn chewed his thumb at once in order to get secret knowledge about where a cure could be found for Diarmuid. The remedy was to be got only in Cape Clear: to put three drops of water from the Well of the Forbidden Weir on the wound and this would cure it instantly. They made no delay in bringing him directly to the well. When Finn was putting the water on Diarmuid's hand Conán Maol was present, and he had an old grudge against Diarmuid. While Finn was taking the third drop of water from the well: "Ah," said Conán, "those are the jealous hands!"9 The water drained away between the fingers of Finn and Diarmuid choked to death on the instant. They carried him west to the verge of the cliff, and he is buried there; and from that day to this the place is called Diarmuid's Cliff.

'And,' said I, 'there is another cove nearby once named Doontomaush, but what we call it lately is Foilnaluinge—and I'll tell you why. I used to hear old people saying that before a lighthouse was built on the Fastnet Rock a ship, full of timber but with no one on board her, appeared one morning in this cove. When the news spread everywhere the menfolk of the Island went to view the wreck. Even the very man who was looking after the light in Cape Clear—an old army-pensioner from England—was right in the midst of them. I suppose he imagined that there was no one on the Island who could match him in knowledge, but anyhow he enquired—as a kind of prank or joke—if there was any man present who would set the sails on the vessel and prepare her for the sea. It happened that a sailor, named Ciarán Daith, was at home after returning from a sea voyage. He stood on the edge of the cliff and stuck his hands in his pockets and began to order men about as would any ship's captain. He commanded them to haul the anchors, to set every sail as he named them one after another, and he

certainly knew his business. Well! when she was out of the
cove and in proper trim and shape for the sea he turned to the
gentleman who put the question to them at the outset and said :
"There she is now after putting out to sea on my orders, and let
you now order her to return and bring her to anchor!" Not a
tittle of a word came from his mouth, but he put his hands
under the tails of his coat and set off for home as rapidly as he
could do it, for the sailor had beaten him hollow although that
certainly wasn't how he imagined things would turn out. All
the old people I heard telling that story were actually present
on the occasion. They claimed that there was something eerie
about that ship for there wasn't trace or tidings of her in the
morning. There were about twenty men of the same age growing
up together in Cape Clear and they were called the contem-
poraries because they were born in the Year of the Ship.'

'What do you call that long headland which is furthest north
on the western end of the Island?'

'That is Ardatroha Point, and situated south-west of it is
Foiladda. There is another spot there on the north side between
Baylnaguygeh and Droumancupoord that people call Reenardnagaorach. I heard that a horse with a rider on his back leaped
out from the land while fleeing from Cromwell's soldiers and
that he landed at Ardnagaorach Head—the marks of the horse-
shoes can still be seen on the rock. With the second jump he
got to the top of the cliff, and the place where he jumped is
called "The Leap of Dashing Donal's Horse". The old folk used
to say that that horseman was a priest in flight.

'There's a fine lake also in the west of the Island and it covers
two acres of land. From this lake a small stream runs down to
Baylnaguygeh and we will go to look at it before you leave the
Island. The evening is far advanced now; have we any thought
at all of going home today?'

'I wouldn't ever ask to leave this place,' he said, 'for it is like
being in Tír na nÓg to be there; neither cold, nor thirst, nor
hunger would affect a man.'

'Upon my soul, good fellow, friars cannot live on texts and
our bellies would be empty if we remained yarning here too
long.'

'As we have burned a nail's breadth of the candle we might

76

as well go the whole way and burn a finger's breadth,' he objected. 'Could you give me any account of the reason why that *carn* of stones is there on the top of the hill?'

'I'll tell you what I heard. A big battle was fought on the hill long ago, and a chieftain fell in the fight. He was buried on the summit of the hill on which we are standing, and the *carn* of stones was built over his grave. His name was Tonn, and that is the reason, why Quarantine Hill got its name "Cnoc Charn Toinn", which means the "Hill of Tonn's Carn". It is easier to believe the explanation, I suppose, than to go looking for witnesses who can produce the evidence. At any rate it looks as if many a one added a stone to his *carn,* for I suppose they thought him worthy of it.'

'Yes indeed,' he said. 'One more question before we leave the hill : what do you call that mountain on the mainland north of the bay, the one that has the big, deep gap at its eastern end?'

'Well,' I said, although I had reached the limit of my endurance for I was exhausted from the day and in dire need of my dinner, 'that is Mount Gabriel, and there is a hole in the top of that mountain which is called Poulanine. The gap that you see is Barna an Cleeve. Do you see those small blue knobs as far off as your eye can see north through that gap? Well, those are the Black Reeks of MacGillacuddy and it's only one out of a hundred days it would be clear enough to catch sight of them from this place.'

'Let me alone, man, there's as fine a prospect from this spot today as is to be seen from any part of Ireland. Well now, we'll be moving.'

Because of the easy walk with the slope we didn't notice the journey down, and it was only a short while before we reached the main road at the Cross of the Four Ways. He stood in the middle of the crossroad and said : 'I suppose that these roads would bring one to every corner of the Island?'

'The road east would bring you to Coosadooglish, the road west to the harbour at Trakieran, the road south to South Harbour, and this one leads down to the strand of Foilcoo— and that's our road home.'

'Arooh,' said Cáit when we reached home, 'what has been keeping you all the day? I thought something had happened

77

to you. I'm standing here at the door since dinner-time, my hands over my eyes against the glare of the sun, to see if you were coming.'

'Whist!' said I, 'there's no knowing what overtakes the person who is absent from home.'

'Well look at the sort of dinner I have to put before you,' she said, 'cooked and grown cold so that it is a matter of indifference whether you get it or not, although it is closer now to supper-time than to dinner-time.'

'Even so,' I replied, 'a person without his dinner means two for supper.'

'Hurry up,' she urged. 'You were talking yesterday about making *ríobún* and I have a handful of hardened wheat there waiting for you as I thought ye would be at home far sooner.'

'Never mind about that, it will take us only a minute to grind that when we get to work on it.'

As soon as we had our dinner eaten, and had a smoke, we got the querns ready. Down on the table we placed them. He and I then stood at opposite sides of the table. I put in a 'feed' and we started the work. We were progressing well : putting in the grain while the meal came out smooth and well-ground.

'If you were to get careless about what you were doing,' I said, 'and failed to put the grain in at regular intervals, it would be very hard work to turn the quern.'

'And why so?'

'Because a "feed" must be kept inside at all times in order to keep the querns apart.'

'Do you always call the fistful of wheat you take out of the dish a "feed"?'

'Yes; and in olden times when the last of the wheat was ground the coarse meal that was scattered around outside the quern was taken and put into the querns again to grind it more finely. That was called "the chaff-feed", the most troublesome of all to turn the quern on from beginning to end of the work; as the old saying has it : "The chaff-feed is the one that weakens the women".'

It didn't take us long to finish the job.

'Now,' I said, 'the morning's milk is the best for making *ríobún* because it is sweeter to taste when made with that than

78

when it is made with the hot milk straight from the cow. Get us some milk, Cáit, and cups and spoons so that we can eat some of what we have made.'

I blended a full cup of the *ríobún,* and I handed it to my friend; and I took the same amount myself.

'Arooh,' he said, 'that's delicious eating, and I'm not a bit surprised that the men who used to eat that sort of food long ago were such splendid, strong, and sturdy fellows.'

'Ah, I can tell you that,' I said, 'they suffered little from toothache at that time whatever about today.'

He went out to look about him and it wasn't long till he came in with something in his hand.

'What kind of a thing is that, and what use was made of it?'

'That's another one of the old implements,' I answered, 'a beetle or pounder. When the "sugawns" were being put on houses long ago the straw had to be pounded with a beetle first before they could be made. Then one person used to feed the straw and another twist it with a little wire crook or "thraw-hook", until they had made a large ball of "sugawn" big enough to fill your arms. A part of it was doubled and this double one was the foundation "sugawn" which was attached to pegs stuck in the walls all the way round under the eaves. The work was carried on like that from gable to gable leaving a space of a foot between every two "sugawns". When that was completed the job of fixing "sugawns" across the roof was begun at one end, leaving about the same distance between them. Their ends were also attached to the bonding "sugawn" which ran right round the house.

'Were it not that the bonding "sugawns" were there it would be necessary to weight the cross ones with good bulky stones.

'When that much was done you would imagine that the entire roof of the house was a window with numerous lights. I myself well remember that work being done, and it was often I twisted a "sugawn", or fed the twister, or attached them to roofs.'10

'Weren't the people of that time very dexterous?' he said. 'They were able to do every sort of work.'

'They were, indeed, for there were no special craftsmen for the work so that they were all handy at doing every kind of job that came their way. Another example is the following : every house had an osier garden attached to it, for considerable use was made of the rods or twigs at that time. A "rishawn" was made of them and that was the only table they had for the potatoes. "Sheehogues" also; and these were used for picking the potatoes from the ridges at harvest time. "Kleevawns" and "sharragawns", both commoner baskets used for general purposes, were also made from the osier twigs. And, finally, pots or creels with wooden bottoms were made out of them in order to hold top-loads on a horse or donkey, for there were no butts then or any thought of them.'

'Didn't the poor people have a troublesome life then,' he said, 'in comparison with today when they have every opportunity and convenience they could ask for?'

'Yes musha, and look at the roads they have today besides the narrow, neglected paths the people had before. But then life does not remain equally and unalterably hard on poor people for ever.'

'I think we have finished what we set out to do today,' I said.

'Yes, and a good day's work. Where do you plan that we should go tomorrow?'

'We will go south-west to Ineer and north on Conaire road through the Cummer until we get as far as Ballyieragh Lake; then across the fields to the castle of Doonanore; back from the west then along the tops of the cliffs to Trakieran, and then up the steep road of Lackavuar and, availing of every short-cut, eastwards through Lissomona until we get home. And now it is time for us to give all our limbs a rest till morning comes again.'

CHAPTER ELEVEN

More stories: The 'preacher'; Loch Errul; The Gruagach
and the Amadán; St Kieran; Finín Mac Gearailt. Milling
and flax-growing in former times. — My visitor departs.

The morning was squally in itself, and the day looked colder
than the previous ones. I took a big wollen cravat down from the
crook to twist it around my neck, for I thought the day wouldn't
be very hot.

'My dear Conchúr,' he said, 'where did you buy that splendid
cravat and what did it cost?'

'It only cost a fourpenny-bit, and I could tell you a story
about it and the place I bought it. A spell of years ago, that is
when I was at the fishing, it happened that a boat used to come
over from London to sell such things to the fishermen : cravats,
mittens, stockings, knitted caps, and everything that would
provide comfort for them and keep them warm in the bad
weather at night. He even had tobacco for sale at ten pence a
pound. Apart only from the tobacco he was able to sell everything he had in the harbour, but he had to haul the anchor
and go well outside the harbour's mouth in order to sell that.
He used heave to there, and when the fishing boats were heading seawards a punt from every boat used to head for him to
buy a week's supply of tobacco, for they would only get enough
for the week every Monday, that is a half-pound a man. One
day when we came close to him three of us entered the punt
and went alongside. No sooner were we there than my two
comrades jumped on board and I had to take care of the punt
for fear it would be smashed against the side of the vessel. I
wasn't long so when one of the officers leaned over the side and
spoke to me from above : "The evening is cold enough," he
said. "It is," I replied, "would you have any drop of whiskey
that you would give a fisherman to warm him on a freezing
night?" "I haven't then," he said, "for, we don't keep the like
of that aboard at all." "You couldn't have a better thing than
a drop of it in time of need," I remarked. He turned away from
me and it wasn't long until he returned and held out a broad
piece of strong thick paper wide open. "Look at that!" he said.

81

"I don't see anything strange or wonderful," I answered. "That is a painting," he said, "and don't you see that shadow the colour of fire, and that stream flowing into it? That is the road the drunkard who is craving for spirits will travel." "Don't believe it," I said, "the person who would only drink a small drop when he was in need of it would never travel that road at all." "I can't help you so," he said, "but I will give you three pounds a year if you only sign your name in this book I have here and promise that you will never again taste another drop of whiskey." "Well that's a thing I won't do," I said firmly. Indignantly he left me, and thanks be to God I am making some sort of living since without the three pounds a year. He used to come back every year and it was from the same fellow that I bought the cravat afterwards for a fourpenny-bit. Let us be off now for we have a long road before us.'

'Don't be out as late as ye were yesterday,' Cáit called after us.

'We won't if we can help it. I assure you.'

We started walking, and when we reached the Cross of the Four Ways he said, 'Where will we go now?' 'We'll head south-west,' I replied. We kept on walking and conversing at the same time, he putting the questions and I answering as well as I was able to. We reached the schoolhouse in a short while and I told him what it was.

'It's a fine schoolhouse,' he said.

'It is even better than that,' I said, 'because there are teachers in that school as good as you would meet in your travels, for indeed it is many the scholar who left that school to enter colleges in Dublin and in other places besides.'

'That will tell you positively that the teachers are good.'

We were walking downhill all the time until we arrived at Tra Ineer and turned north the Conaire road, a grand level road cut out of the hillside for its whole length along the edge of the harbour. That brought us into the Cummer.

'There's a grand cluster of houses,' he remarked. 'And so this is the place you call the Cummer.'

'That is what it is called today but I heard that it had a different name long ago—Glensmole. Do you see the two hills, one east the other on the west side? There was a wood growing on the side of each and the trees were so high that their bran-

82

ches were intertwined over the glen in the way that going through Glensmole then was like passing under a bridge.

'Is the lake very far from us?' he asked.

'No, about a quarter of a mile more.'

When we got as far as the lake we stopped and he enquired if there were any trout in it, or any other kind of fish.

'No wisha, neither trout nor salmon, but freshwater eels are there in plenty. I hear that there are little worms there called *cúóga,* and I often heard that, after spending twenty-four hours in the water any sort of wooden vessel, no matter how dirty, would be as clean and gleaming as the day the craftsman lifted his hand from it after the finishing touch, for those *cúóga* would pick at and polish clean everything on it, both inside and out; but if a garment were forgotten on washing day and left behind in it, neither trace nor tidings of it would ever be found again because those worms would completely devour it.'[1]

We took the short-cut northwards over the hill and headed for Ardacushlaun Cliff. And a high cliff it is in all earnest, standing absolutely perpendicular, with the old castle straight across from it looking like an island, although some years ago a nice little level road of green inch-land lead into it; but now today it is broken, smashed, and torn down because of tempest and storm so that you could hardly cross by it.[2]

'It wouldn't be any surprise if there were old and wonderful stories linked with that castle,' he said.

'There are enough and plenty—more than I could tell you— even of those I myself heard about it. Let us sit here a while.'

'There was a man living in that place long ago whom they used call the Gruagach of Doonanore : I imagine no one has any knowledge of how long it is since he was there. It was said that he was enchanted. There was a guard, called the Amadán Mór, on his wife and the castle, and the Gruagach put him under a test one day to see if he was absolutely loyal to him.

' "Well," said he, "I am going on a visit and I won't be returning for two or three days; don't allow anyone inside the door until I come back."

' "Don't fear that I will," said the Amadán Mór.

'The Gruagach set out and instead of crossing the sea he went hunting to Glensmole. The Amadán stretched himself out across the door and with the heat of the sun sleep overtook him. The Gruagach wasn't long away before he came back again, and anyone who ever saw him wouldn't recognise him for he altered his appearance and his features by magic. The Amadán Mór was in a sound sleep before him and didn't notice him entering. Once inside he turned on his heel and struck the Amadán with a belt of his boot.

' "Sit up out of that sleepy-head," he shouted.

'The sight of the Amadán's eyes spread with amazement when he saw the stranger standing inside on the floor. At that same moment the lady of the castle who was sitting near the fire cried out: "Amadán, don't let that fellow out before you discover the why and the wherefore about him."

'The Amadán lifted his sword from the threshold where he was stretched out for himself when he was asleep. The stranger was not to be outdone and drew out his own sword against him. The two of them set to at one another with the swords and the stranger was getting the upper hand of the doorkeeper; it wasn't long before the Amadán Mór lost a leg from the knee down.

' "Now," said the stranger, "will you let me out?"

' "Indeed I won't," said the Amadán as he continued fighting all the time.

'It was short until he lost a part of his other leg but he didn't flinch or give in. The stranger then said : "I'll put one of your legs back under you but let me out," and he did so; but it was the same story always—the Amadán wouldn't let him out. "I'll give you the other leg back if you let me pass," the stranger offered. "I'll get back my other leg, one way or another, or cut off your head, for you will stay here until the Gruagach of Doonanore comes home and you pay for kissing his wife."

'Then it was that the Gruagach revealed his true identity to him by blowing away the magic that was on him, and the Amadán recognised who he had at once.

' "I beg your pardon, Master," he said, "I never dreamed it was you were there."

' "It is granted, and I am very thankful to you," he replied, "for I see that you are as faithful to me as the bark is to the tree."

'And now do you see the high cliff on the other side of the cove?' I asked. 'I heard that there was merchandise coming from foreign parts to the Gruagach during his time. Into that cove there, called Coosadoona, the goods were brought for unloading. And there's every sign that they used to do so for there are large iron rings bolted into the rock on the southern side of the cove and it was to those that the ships used to be tied up. They are to be seen there still at the ebb of a big tide.

'That's my account for you of the Gruagach and of the castle of Doonanore. I wonder did you hear what the poet said :

> You will get the goblet never emptied yet,
> You will get the horn and the hound for sport
> That the Gruagach owned in Doonanore,
> Though he's loathe to give it to your sort.'[3]

'Do you remember that old castle's being in any better state than we see it now?'

'That's how it has been always, as far as I can remember at any event, but I heard that it was in Carew's time that the breach you see there was made by a shell from a big gun fired from the top of Foilard.[4] Let us move on eastwards and keep shortening the road.'

We travelled on from the west to Traleagig and through Coomnakille until we emerged on the path at the end of the graveyard.

'That is the graveyard called Killkieran,' I said, 'and there's Kieran's church inside in the centre of the graveyard. It is said that it is one of the oldest churches in Ireland and that Kieran himself was one of the elders of the Irish saints. We'll go in to look at the whole place.'

We did so and we went into the old church too.

'Did you hear where Kieran was born?'

'I have been hearing all my life that he was born in Cape Clear, and signs on the fifth of March every year is kept as a holy day on the Island in his honour ever since, and I'm certain that it will be as long as anyone lives there. Another thing I used to hear old people saying was that if a mad dog bit anyone who was born under Kieran's protection he wouldn't do a bit of harm to him and the cut wouldn't fester.'

'Ah' he said, 'he had the powers.'

'Yes,' I said, 'in every way. I heard that when he was over on the mainland that he met a particular woman in the course of his travels. She was a woman who didn't like her husband and who would prefer seeing him buried to getting a barrel of seed. This is what she said :

> O illustrious Kieran who lives west in Clear
> I ask you how I should kill my man?

'Answering her he said :

> Use fine white flour and the fairly-hot milk of a sheep
> And give it to him daily at the tail-end of its heat.'

'Arooh,' said my comrade, 'isn't that what would nourish him instead of killing him?'

'Of course it is,' I replied, 'for you know well that he wouldn't give wicked advice to anyone but counsel of the most virtuous sort.'

'It's a grand spot he chose to build his church, there at the edge of the harbour on the level part of the slope.'

'Yes, as the poet said when he passed by :

> In cosy Conaire where the sun shone well
> 'Twas there blessed Kieran first made his cell.'

When we had examined every part of the place and were leaving in the direction of the gate, he noticed a headstone on one of the graves with a lot of writing on it. He stopped and read the inscription.

'Did you hear who wrote that? The one who made it had a gifted hand and great intelligence.'

'His name was Finín Mac Gearailt, that very man I referred to already.'

'Is it there that man is buried?' he asked.

'No, musha, but west in America for before the Famine came he said that "hunger without want would come and war without fear" and that neither of them would catch him in Ireland. It was true for him : they didn't.'

'That was like a prophecy,' he said, 'seeing that he had secret knowledge of what was about to happen.'

86

'It was. There was no tradesman's craft that he wasn't skilled in; and I heard that after giving him seven weeks schooling the master wasn't able to teach him any more.'

'God's blessing on the souls of the dead,' we said as we were leaving and closing the gate after us.

We went south by the top of the strand until we got as far as the 'gallawns'. 'That is the memorial stone that we call Gallán Kieran,' I said, 'and it is easy to recognise it for the mark of his hands are clearly visible on it today, as clearly as on the day they were made. There's a streamlet flowing down to the strand from it and it is called Tubberkieran's stream. The people visit the "gallawns" on the night of St Kieran's feastday to pray, and they take some of the water home with them. Indeed many is the fisherman in the past who knelt down at the stream and drank from it on his way past. The road home from this place is steep and rugged, and you know that we mustn't draw yesterday's reproach down on us.'

We climbed up the Lackavuar, and then northwards along the road from the west, that is the Chapel road. Where we reached the top of the Lacka there is green-swarded lea-land on the left side inside the ditch, and I remarked that I often heard that Kieran's people had a house there that he was born and reared in.

'I'm pleased to hear that,' he said, 'and that I will be able to tell that I saw the spot in which the Elder of the Saints of Ireland was born.'[5]

All the while we were climbing uphill until we reached the Chapel. Naturally we went in for to say a few prayers. When we came out he stopped in order to look about him, and said : 'It's a nice Chapel. Ye must be very Irish-minded in this Island for everything I saw inside in the way of writing was entirely in Irish.'

'Irish is the native speech we ever had and still have besides.'

'Do you know how long that Chapel is built?' he asked.

'I couldn't say the year but I'll tell you what I heard. When I was only a garsoon I remember hearing some old people, who were very advanced in years saying that they recalled a thatched Chapel being in that hollow to the south-east before the new Chapel was put up where it is now. I myself recall that bell on

87

top of the gable being put there. Let's not delay any longer but head straight home.'[6]

'Ah,' said Cáit on our reaching the house, 'fear is a great charm!'

'To tell you the truth,' said I, 'we walked twice as far today : we were as far west as the "Flase Men".'

'By rights ye should be tired enough after the day; I suppose ye won't go out again until tomorrow.'

'Indeed we will,' I said, 'we have to make another journey; we'll go to look at the little mill after our dinner.'

We took it easy for a spell for we were exhausted, after the long tramp during the time before dinner. But we hadn't far to go this time : about a ten minute walk. When we reached the place I showed him the quern first of all.

'That looks,' he said, 'as if no human hand ever turned it, for it seems far too heavy for that.'

'I used to hear that it was the stream there falling down over the ledge that used turn it, and indeed its name is "The Stream of the Little Mill".'

'I can't make out any trace of the remains of a house there,' he said.

'Come over here a while. Can't you see that that place seems to be a sort of wall built by human hand at some time?'

'I see; you are right.'

'Another thing I heard about it was that the way one paid the miller was to give him a little of the meal in return for his work. I suppose it was so long ago that no money at all was being minted; for I never heard any old man saying that he had any account of when the mill was there.'

'But all the same,' he said, 'there's solid proof of its existence : it was there at some time. Is any use made of that place now?'

'Yes,' I said, 'when there's a scarcity of water that place always has a supply and you can see that it is used for washing clothes. When flax was planted by people long ago they used to pond it there after it was cut.'

'Is that sort of work in the Island at all nowadays?'

'No wisha, but it is one of the earliest memories of mine seeing flax growing in Cape Clear, and coarse homespun cloth being made out of it.'

'That occupation should be kept going always,' he said, 'because it is a very profitable and beneficial business, and it was once very widespread all over Ireland and a great source of money.'

'And the way the world looks now that activity will be as extensive again as it ever was, with the help of God. However, as the man who first said it put it : "Let us do our share and earn our fare." We can't live on hopes.'

The sun was ripening into yellow before sinking.

'Well,' he said, 'I'm thinking about being on my way tomorrow.'

'Arooh, haven't you plenty of time! Stay a few more days.'

'I must go : I have no choice,' he said. 'If the day happens to be so windy that the boat will not be able to go out, I'll have to go to the Post Office and speak on the 'phone to make my excuses.'

I laughed my fill when I heard what he said. He gazed at me in bewilderment.

'What's making you laugh?'

'Alas! I'm truly sorry for you, there's no telephone in Cape Clear and I suppose there never will be.[7] There's no news of any kind, neither story to tell nor poem to recite, going from or coming to the Island except by the post alone, and it is often I remember the place being without the post even for a fortnight in winter because a boat wouldn't live in the mad seas.'

Ambasa, that wasn't how it was on the following morning, but fine, calm, and sunny.

He left us, and I got neither tale, trace nor tidings from him since. He has kept discreetly silent up to this about everything I told him, and I'm thankful to him. But when he will see this story in print yet he'll strike his thigh with his palm and that very moment he'll recall his visit to Cape Clear. And, indeed, I could tell him much more than I did at that time if he were to come to see me again.

CHAPTER TWELVE

*I have silenced many a mumbling nit-wit
during a* scoraíocht. *Some tales I told recently.*

Three or four of the neighbours' boys came into my place one
night on a *scoraíocht*. When the long winter nights arrive there
is no pastime, or any other diversion for boys on this Island
apart from a visit for gossiping and yarning, especially in a
house where there would be an old man, in order to listen to his
ancient lore and old tales.

'You're welcome boys! I didn't see you with a week.'

'No one could stick his head out his door in that time,' said
Pádraig, 'for the nights were too dark. Tonight won't be black
at all for the moon is up at nightfall.'

'God prosper you,' said Mícheál, 'you're doing something.'

'I'm making a "sugawn" chair for myself for ye know I'm
getting old, and I'm making this now in order to sit at my ease
in it on the hob beside the fire.'

'When you'll have that made and are seated comfortably in
it I'm sure you would be capable of giving wise decisions to a
host of people,' said Pádraig.

'Give over your mockery and lend me a hand instead; make
little tie-rolls for me and I assure ye that when I have it made
and my bones are snug and comfortable, I'll tell ye all the
stories I ever heard about pookas and *síofraí.*'

'Good enough,' said Mícheál, 'we'll give you every help we
can. A man can work and talk at the same time.'

'Well, boys,' I started, 'it is often I heard that the loneliest
places out and out are beside the sea and the strands. I heard
a man saying that there were four men fishing in a boat and
that it was very late in the night when they came ashore on the
strand. The tide was quite low; he said that it was at half-ebb
when they rowed the boat hard on to the strand. They dragged
her up out of the water a distance of her own length, but if
their life depended on it they couldn't budge her another inch.

' "We're wearing ourselves out," they said to one another.
"We'll redden a pipe and have a smoke, and then we'll try
it again."

'They did so, and tried once again, but it was the same story : she was just as if she was bolted to the strand, they couldn't get a move or stir out of her. But the man who was telling me the story said that he first looked about him on the strand, and then up at the top of the cliff.

' "Well," said he, "it is many a man stood on this strand in the past, and where are they all tonight that they wouldn't come and give us some help in drawing up the boat along with us?"

'No sooner had he uttered that much than they heard the chuckling, and the fits of laughter, and a great buzz of chatter on the top of the cliff. "There's no need for ye to be making fun of us, but let ye come down and help us to haul the boat so that we won't be here till morning!"

'At that same moment they heard the tramp of feet coming down in their direction, and you'd think from it that if there was one there there were a hundred. When they heard them coming they said to one another. "She isn't a boat without hauling now"; but what happened was that fright gripped them for they didn't see anyone but themselves around the boat.

' "Let us try her again," said one of them, "to see what we are able to do, for I imagine that the laughing crowd a while back will be no help at all to us."

'They pressed forward towards the boat again and up she went without a halt more quickly than they could walk, until she was hauled to the top of the grassy bank so that there was no more to be done except to put "legs" under her, and tie a rope to the stake and she would then be safe from a storm.'

'You know of course,' said Pádraig, 'that they weren't people of this world.'

'Of course they weren't,' I said, 'for if they were they would see them. They wanted a bit of fun at first and then to lend a helping hand when it suited their book to do so. Those people are everywhere—except that we don't see them—just like they were there on that night.'

'What you'll do is scare the wits out of us with your vivid storytelling,' said Mícheál, 'in the way that dread won't allow us to go on the strand or to sea again.'

'If that little tale scares you it is easy to make you afraid, and

91

so I've told you the last of my stories about *síofraí.*'

'Don't mind those "dailteens", old fellow,' said Donncha. 'It is to the stories about the strangest eeriest things that I like to be listening for, while I know that there are people who are more fearful than others, as far as I am concerned that sort of tale wouldn't frighten me at all.'

'I know that,' I said, 'for I remember a night I myself and two others were fishing in a small boat. It was a fine night and fish were there for the catching until the dawn. Our little boat was pretty full of fish about midnight, and we said to one another that we had better head for the strand and land our fish, then go home to eat a bit of supper and come back again and, since the night was so fair, go out again with the change of light at dawn. We did what we said. Two of us were travelling the one road home for we lived near one another, and our companion had to take a different route to get home. The last word of conversation we had together while we were parting was that we would make no delay at home but be back as quickly as we could. When we had a bit of supper eaten the two of us returned to the little boat but, despite all the haste we made the other man was before us on the strand.

' "You weren't long," I said, "although you had a longer walk than we had, and did you have any feeling of lonesomeness going or coming?"

' "Wisha I didn't," he answered, "I considered that if I were a good Christian in God's sight that I needn't fear; and that gave me confidence." '

'Ah,' said Ciarán, 'he certainly had strong faith.'

'I wonder are there any *síofraí* at all there,' I remarked. 'For maybe it is the way people imagine things of that kind in their own minds. It's a long time since I myself and two others were after returning one night from the fish-market. We moored our boat in the harbour. Two of us had a long way to go and the third man's journey wasn't so long. He took to his road and we both set out for home together. I had to travel twice as far as my companion. When he came as far as his own house he went in home from me. Well, I was absolutely alone then and it was the dead of night; still it was a bright moonlit night as I kept on walking. There was a certain place on the road that had the name of being lonesome, and when I thought about that a great feeling of nervousness came over me. But before I got as far as that place there was a ditch on the side of the road that had bushes of french furze growing on it. As I was getting close to that place I heard the loveliest music ever. I stood still. It seemed to me that a host of small birds was singing right there in the air on the tops of the bushes. It appeared odd to me at that time of night when by right the birds of the air should be asleep. I got such a start that I thought every single rib of hair on my head was standing bolt upright. I didn't follow that road any farther but turned in over the ditch and took every short-cut possible to my home; and I'll warrant ye that much grass didn't grow under my feet for my limbs were sinewy and supple at the time whatever about today.'

'There used to be a show of apparitions and of eerie things happening long ago,' said Donncha.

'Oh, they used certainly say that,' I said. 'When I was young I heard an old fellow saying that a man was coming home one night, and that he was passing through a place that had the reputation of being lonesome, and that he imagined that he got a prod in his shoulder-blade from behind him. He turned around because he thought that there was someone walking behind him who had given him the blow in the back. He paid no further attention to it on his way home nor for the rest of the night. How was it in the morning with him but that he couldn't leave his bed and, instead of getting better it was worse he was becoming. Everyone was saying that he had got a fairy blow.

'At that time there was an odd person here and there who had some secret knowledge of complaints of that sort and who were able to make potions and medicines that would cure the victim. And it was said that the reason they had those powers was that they themselves were familiar with the fairy host. One of them was sent for to come to this man to see if he could do him any good. He asked the messenger how he was complaining, and he told him what happened to the patient and where it occurred. "I understand fully now," he said, "and he got out of it lightly in escaping being killed outright, for the fool of the fairy host threw a black river-stone at him and, if it had struck him in the heart he would have been finished. I'll let him have a herbal cure." He gave the messenger a bottle-full of the stuff he had compounded himself. "Here," he said, "and take good care of yourself and don't break your bottle, for I'm certain that if the same lot meet you on the way it is to be feared that, if they can at all, they will be watching to trip you and smash the bottle." Ambasa, he did his job well; and true enough for the maker of the medicine the sick man had only taken half the stuff when he was in possession of his old vigour and strength as fully as he ever was any day in his life.'

'It's only a short while ago,' said Ciarán, 'since you said that you didn't believe in *síofraí* at all, yet they must have been very plentiful long ago if we are to credit what the old people say.'

'I don't know,' I said, 'but in any event what you say about the old people is true; and indeed they told about even stranger things : that skeins of linen thread used to be seen being spread out on the stone fences after the sun had gone down, but that they didn't see those who were putting them there at all—only the hands and fingers fixing and arranging the thread on the ditches; and remember that the twilight hour was the proper time for bringing in such skeins instead of putting them out. I can tell you that those were the ditches that used to get a clear berth from then until morning.'

'It's a great wonder Conchúr,' said Pádraig, 'that fear allowed anyone to put his head outside his door at all at that time from the moment the night fell.'

'Well,' said I, 'this is how things are, there have always been timorous people and fearless people, and there always will be. I don't know in the world why it is but people see things that they imagine are preternatural; yet it happens in the long run that it isn't so.'

'And what use is it for you to be talking?' said Pádraig, 'people don't change. There are those who would say that apparitions are to be seen on the sea as well as on land.'

'Yes,' I agreed, 'it is said that there is no kind of animal on the land that its like isn't to be found in the sea. There's the dog-fish, and there's no difference between him and a dog except that he hasn't any ears. Then there are the cat-fish, the sea-pigs, the sea-horses and sea-cows.[1] If it comes down even to the mermaid, she exists. Do you see Illauneanna up there? I heard old people saying that a mermaid was seen at the western end of that island with the sun shining on her on an evening when the wind was from the east; she had a comb in her hand and was dressing her hair. They used to say then that the seal was the mermaid's brother.'

'And here is another tale I used to hear being told by the old people : There was a boat from Cape Clear fishing off the coast long ago on a fine summer's morning. It was so calm that the water was like glass. They saw this brown white-backed cow coming towards them as she moved on the surface of the sea from the north-west. She didn't stop until she stuck her head in over the stern of the boat. Naturally all who were aboard became frightened. After a short while she left them and headed back on the same course from which she had come. Their amazement was all the greater when they saw her coming again on the next morning. She did the very same thing : she put her head in over the stern. After a while she left again as she had come. When they saw her coming on the third morning they couldn't be more surprised if the sky fell on the land. While she acted in the same way she remained much longer than she did on the other mornings, as if she were expecting someone to speak to her or to do something for her. But at last she turned away from the boat and let out three bellows so that you could hear her throughout all the lands. It was reported that she had an udder as big as a basket as she walked on the surface of the sea with her paps touching it as she moved. "We've seen enough now," they all said to one another, "let us make for home and not stay here any longer." I heard that they told the tale to the priest afterwards and what he said was that they were the cowardly craven men to say that none of them had the courage to catch one of her horns.'

95

'Upon my word,' said Ciarán, 'if he were in the boat himself he'd be nervous enough about taking her by the horn. Still, I suppose she didn't intend doing any harm to them, for if so she would have done it.'

'If I were in the boat,' said Pádraig, 'I'd certainly force a confession from her.'

'You would too! Here on the hob you are saying it, and I imagine you were almost paralysed with fear when you heard the story.'

'Have you any other stories apart from those about pookas and *síofraí*?' asked Mícheál.

'I suppose ye never heard about the soldiers,' I said, 'who came to Cape Clear in the time of Cromwell.'

'We didn't wisha,' they said, 'for the love of goodness tell us about them.'

'I heard that a boat came from the east below between Carrigyleyra and the Island, and it full of redcoats. Quite naturally they didn't know where they could come ashore. On their passage west past Doonclayreh they saw men and women inside on the strand washing and gutting fish after landing a catch there. When the soldiers noticed the people on the strand, they themselves turned to enter for they knew that it was a suitable place for a boat to land. When the people saw them coming all but one woman fled. At that time shebeens were numerous all over the Island, and this woman, who hadn't run away with the rest of them had one. The soldiers spoke to her after they landed and asked her where the people they saw there a while past had gone.

' "They hurried away," she said, "for aren't ye soldiers surely? and they became afraid of you."

' "Isn't it small fear you had of us in comparison with others?"

' "What use was it for me to show lack of courage?" she replied, "here I am and you can kill me if you want to."

' "You have a gentleman's word, good woman," said the man in command of them, "that nothing at all will happen to you since you were so courageous as to stand your gound."

'The woman invited them to go along with her. They hadn't

96

far to go before they reached the woman's house. What did she do then but take out her jar and give each man a *taoscán* of whiskey. That was the time that white whiskey, or poteen, was sixpence a quart. They thanked her and went straight out the door. They weren't so well-beloved and innocuous in any other house in the Island into which they went : they did a world of damage and destruction. Everyone fled. They didn't leave a cream-crock or milk-pot that they didn't spill their contents all over the floor. With their knives they cut up the fish that were dried and cured in boxes into little pieces just as a hawk would. They slashed the bags of winnowed grain and scattered it all over the floor. Any cattle that came their way they docked their tails for there was no one bold enough to say "beware of the pooka" to them. After they had spent the day in that way and done an enormous amount of damage, they were making their way back to their boat. They didn't forget to call into the woman who showed them the kindness in the morning. Likely enough it was for her own good that she gave each of them another drink. They thanked her and went off with some show of gratitude and without doing a farthings worth of harm to anything that belonged to her. What is that you're saying Pádraig?'

'I'm saying that the people of the Island at that time were a cowardly lot to allow a dozen little soldiers to trample on them and do such damage without giving them a fine hammering and battering for themselves.'

'One would think from you that you would do such wonders as make a cat with two tails; but only think of it: if you were to see a soldier with a gun heading for you and you having nothing but your two hands hanging from you, you would go into an auger-hole from him if you were able to; so you can see that it is easy for the man who isn't playing at all to be a good gambler. The house in which the soldiers got the drink that day is still standing. For a long time after that there was terror in the hearts of the people for fear they would fall on them by day or by night. A woman opened the door of her house on a night that was black, raw, and windy : "Ah," she said, "Cape Clear is a safe garrison tonight.[2] There's no fear of the soldiers coming at any rate." "Watch out for yourself," said the voice of a man who was standing right in front of the door, "I am here," and what was he but a soldier!'

'Redden the pipe,' said Pádraig, 'and pass it round before we leave.'
'Do you smoke tobacco, child?'
'I would if I could get it.'

'The smoke of a pipe into your moutheen
It is wrong for you to draw,
But with a thorn-stick your ribs should be beaten
For starting to smoke at all

'Off home with ye now for it won't be long till the moon is down and it will be dark, and one feels more fear on a dark night than on a bright one. When tomorrow night comes we'll be describing old customs, and talking about the pipers and dances that were there at that time and about a great many other things ye haven't heard yet.'
'For a small head,' said Donncha, 'your's holds an amazing amount of knowledge!'
'Out with ye now and be off home, and give over joking, for it has ever been said that the fortunate have their fun at the expense of the unfortunate.'

CHAPTER THIRTEEN

More stories from the old days — Pastimes — Weddings.

When they came to my place on the following night I said to
them that great changes had taken place in the world in every
way.

'Whatever about the present day,' I said, 'in those times we
have been talking about there was nothing with which to bake
the cake of bread. What caused me to refer to that is that cake
I see there baked in the "bastible".

'Although I don't remember it, but only as I heard it, there
used to be a four-cornered baking stone in every house. The
stone was placed in a standing position in front of the fire,
and the cake was made in exactly the same shape as the stone.
The cake was then placed on its edge on the hearth and
supported by the stone. It was left there until the fire made a
hard crust on that side. Then the other side was turned towards
the fire and given the same treatment. They used to be turning
and twisting it in that way until it was fit to eat. You should
realise that there was a support at the back of the stone which
kept it standing; but for that the job couldn't be done properly.

'That was how it was long ago : they hadn't any such con-
veniences as they have today. I myself remember the coming of
other appliances such as the griddles—those were flat slabs of
iron that had two grips on them. The griddle used to be hung by
a hook from the pot-rack, or crane, over the fire. About a
quarter of an inch thick it was, with a right side and a wrong,
and it was smooth and shiny. A cake the size of the griddle was
made, and after it was made it was cut into four quarters. When
the griddle was hot enough the cake was placed in it. Whenever
each quarter was ready for turning it was turned so separately,
for that was the most convenient way of doing it : a full-sized
cake couldn't be turned in a griddle.

'But not every single house had a griddle, and so the woman
of a house without one of them used to go looking for the loan
of one from the wife of a neighbour. It didn't take long, however, until there was one of them in every house throughout the
Island; and for many a long year that was the method they

99

used in order to bake a cake. If a man got on well in life, another fellow would say of him : "Ah, that one can sell his griddle for his loaf is baked."[1]

'But you yourselves are grown-up and sensible enough to know well the change that has come over the world. That change has affected every sort of thing : food, drink, clothes, music, dancing and—if I say so—the very speech of the people too.

'I remember that when I myself was a pretty hardy garsoon, pipers used to come into the Island here. You can well say that those were the musicians worth listening to. One of them used to give a spell in the Island every year and, of course, St Patrick's Day—for that was a "pattern" day. On that day the old man who used not leave home during the rest of the year would go to drink his "Patrick's pot", and look at the dancers, and listen to the piper. Perhaps he used to meet five or six of his own sort that he hadn't seen for a while before. One of them would say : "Well, neighbours and friends, let us go on in to drink our 'Patrick's pot', for it is seldom we meet, and as the old proverb put it,

Choose your company before you go drinking,
And see what's in your pocket before you walk in!"

They used to sit round a table by themselves at one end of the house. One of them called for a half gallon of beer and the man of the house would put the half gallon in front of them and a glass for each one of them. It cost sixpence a gallon at that time. The man who called the round filled the glasses for the company and they drained them after wishing one another "sláinte". He used to go around once again and the man who got the last drop from the half gallon in his glass without its being filled, the one sharing it out would say to him : "Well, it gave you its passion, but it didn't give you your ration." It was then that man's duty to fill it again. He used to take the half gallon in his hand, knock on the table with it and say, "Now, man of the house, fill this can again for us".

'When each of them had drunk two or three glasses and was merry, one of them would say to another : "Sing us a song". You may well say that he was a very good hand at singing a fine old song in Irish, and when he finished another one would catch him by the hand and say : "Give me your hand, my old friend, we are all one here". Other things that used usually be said to the singer were : "May you get a golden ring as big as a horse's collar !" and "May God not make life hard for you and, if He does may He make it easy for you again." They used to spend a while in that way until they thought it time to get up and go home together.

'The piper used be at the other end of the house, and you can take my word for it that he wouldn't be alone : a party of boys and girls was always there listening to him and dancing to his music. He used to sit in a chair with the bellows under one armpit and the bagpipe under the other. There was a tube protruding from the bellows through which he filled the bagpipes with air. The bagpipe itself had a narrow neck from which stretched a long yellow brass tube called the chanter the end of which was down on his knee. He used to blow up the bellows with his elbow until it was so full of air that it was fit to burst. Then he started to play by moving his fingers along the holes in the pipe. There were other pipe holes called drones in the end of the bag from which there poured a deep heavy hum accompanying the music and making it all the grander.

'Two couples used then move out on to the floor and the piper played a reel and a jig for them; and when they finished that bout of dancing the piper was paid twopence, for that was the reward he got for every spell of dancing that was done. The girls returned to their seats and the two boys used then select another two girls for the next dance. Once again the piper was paid his twopence, and this time the boys stopped dancing and it was then the girls turn to choose two other boys for the next one.

'That was the way the time passed until everyone was half-dead with fatigue. However, if any sign of fading interest in the piper's music was shown so that he wasn't pleased, he began to sulk and would stop playing. He would then get a drink from one of the boys to put him in good humour again. After that he spoke up and said :

> When the piper has downed a drink
> The piper will play a fine jig.

Straightaway the fit of pique was over and he would say:
"Ye are far better than the four a while ago", and in the same
instant he was squeezing the bellows, swelling the bag, and
playing once again with vigour.

'Like hundreds of other things I suppose that a great number
of the old pipers' tunes are also lost.'

'Would you be able to name some of them for us?' Mícheál
asked.

'I heard their names and I still remember some of them:
"The Jolly Tinker", "The Mad Buck-goat", "Sheila Geary",
"The Old Horned Sheep", "The Comely Brown Maiden",
"The Rocky Road", "St Patrick's Day in the Morning", "Old
Bridges", and—the grandest tune of them all—"The Fox-
chase"; listening to that last would send you to sleep. That is
the kind of music I heard and the sort of dancing I saw when
I myself was young; and the whole world knows that it was
finer than that whirling around so common now that would
make my head reel if I were watching it; as the dancers used
to say at that time:

> If I only got a penny for the piper,
> And a fine can of drink for to pour,
> A drop of cold water from a dyke
> Wouldn't trouble my throat any more.[2]

'St Stephen's Day was another "pattern" day among the
people. On that day as well the old folk would go to the public
house. On the same day the boys had a wren, and it would
give you pleasure and comfort to see a party of them going from
house to house reciting their verses in fine Irish at every door,
and never once in English. The custom was that one of them
was appointed to chant the verses. The captain of the party
himself in front, and he had another boy with him who had a
flag on the top of a pole. When they used to reach the door of
every house, one of them knocked at the door if it wasn't open
before them. Then the boy whose duty it was to recite the verses
started:

> We brought you the wren, O mistress of the house,
> And with no desire for porter or for grain,

102

But only with a wish to keep up the diversion
That is the way in our country on St Stephen's Day.

But if they were addressing the man of the house this is what
would be said to him :

We brought you the wren, O beloved friend,
And with no desire for stout or for a gift,
But only with a wish to look for the sport
That is usual in our country the last day of the year.

We brought back the wren from over the sea,
He's on top of a stick and the stiffness of death in him,
He is cursed and cranky and is hard to please
Give us the money or he'll start to abuse you.

They used to get a little hand-offering of money; as the
person put it who first said it : "A small hand-offering is better
than an excuse, no matter how good that is." Then it was that
the people of the house were praised :

We bid ye goodbye, O people of this house,
May none of ye die until ye're very old,
May God grant ye luck in chattels and in children,
And may ye be seven times better with the coming
       of next Christmas,

and at the end of each verse they all shouted "Huzzah". That
is the way we used to spend St Stephen's Day long ago; and
when the day was over we shared out the money we had got
although it wasn't likely that we had any great amount to
divide. Still and all everyone was satisfied coming home in the
evening.'[3]

'We had another custom called a "cohalaun", that is a great
gathering together of all the people; and they had special places
for that—large, smooth, level fields for dancing, with a piper
seated in a corner playing for them. It was in the summer that

these gatherings were held. I know a field that is still called the Piper's Field : it is over there to the east close to Carriglee; but there is only a part of it left now for it has been divided up by the road. The stone seat where the piper used to sit can still be seen today just as it was at that time.

'I recall many old crafts being practised in this Island long ago that the people of the present time have no knowledge of at all. I recall the women spinning the linen thread with their wheels. That done they made the nets out of the thread with the help of a needle and a "skun" or mesh-measurer. Then the "nozzels" were spun and plaited. The rest of the work involved in net-making was done by the men, that is attaching the "nozzels" to the nets and tying those to the haul-ropes. At that time every house in the Island had a spinning-wheel for flax and another one for wool, as well as a pair of carding instruments for hackling or teasing the wool and flax, for there were no machines there then nor any notion that there would be. They used to tease and spin their own wool. When it was spun they wound it into balls of yarn. Half the yarn was made into a warp by putting it on "kippens" stuck in the wall of the house for that purpose. The threads were put around the "kippens" in pairs, and a figure-of-eight cross-tie made on the two ends of the warp for if this was forgotten the weaver couldn't put the yarn into the loom. When that much was done both the warp and the balls of wool were brought to the weaver who did his share of the job before sending the material on to the fuller for tucking or thickening. By then it was properly finished frieze, or what they used to call "household frieze" then which no frieze could be found that had better wearing qualities; as the woman said long ago :

> Good luck to the handling my frieze got,
> Good luck to the work done by slay and loom,
> And to the treadle which gave it fair play.

'Linen cloth was made in the same way, but they got much more trouble in making it than in producing the frieze. Flax-seed was first set in the ground just like any other sort of seed, and when it had grown and was ripe it was pulled and sheaves

104

made of it. Then it was ponded or retted: nine days it spent in the water. After being lifted from the water and spread to dry in the sun it was made into sheaves from which little sheavelets or tufts were pulled, a fistful at a time. These were pounded by a beetle until the husks on the straw were broken and crushed. It was then drawn through the coarse hackle first, and afterwards through the fine one, and in this process stripped of all the coarse tow. Finally every one of the tufts or sheavelets was combed with the clove until it was so smooth and pliant that you would think that it was never straw that once grew in the ground. By that time it was ready for the spinning-wheel. It was spun by this, and the weaver then wove it, just like the frieze, except that this time he produced homespun linen.

'March was their chosen month for bleaching the homespun linen, that is spreading it on the bleach-green and leaving it there under the rain and all kinds of weather, day and night for that whole month, until in the end it was as white as the snow. Then it was stretched out for cutting, and shirts were made of it and bed-sheets: homespun linen sheets, which couldn't be surpassed for their lasting power. It wouldn't surprise me a bit if some remnants of that cloth were to be found in the Island even at this very moment in time.

'All that proves that those living then didn't spend a day of their lives idle. However, those things I have named are made today by machinery in mills, and the one who hadn't the money to come by them would have to go in the want of them, and so would have to carry on without them.'[4]

'There is no talk today of a great number of customs that existed in the past. Take the funeral on its way to the grave-yard: the women used to be wailing the whole length of the way until the coffin was carried into the cemetery. The same "keening" was customary in the house where the wake was held. Whenever a woman related to the family entered she would go up to the plank where the corpse was laid out and burst out into a long tearful lamentation over it. At the same moment all the women already within would stand alongside her and as they all keened together it would cause you anguish to listen to their lamenting and "keening" of the dead person which lasted until they were weary and worn out. I haven't seen or heard women doing that at any funeral for thirty years; and so that is another old custom that has disappeared.

'There is a story, boys, about an old man living long ago who went to say a prayer for an old neighbouring woman who had died. On his way home from the wake house he heard that another old woman was just after dying in another house. Half of his tongue was protruding with the dint of excitement while he was telling his own old wife that this particular old woman was dead.

' "She is too," she said.

' "There are two Deaths there so since two are dead together," he said. "Upon my word but I thought that there was only one Death there!" '[5]

'Arooh, give over that sort of talk,' said Mícheál, 'and tell us something about matchmaking and marriages that will raise our spirits so that we won't be lonesome going home.'

'I'll tell ye how I used to see the way in which matches were arranged. As you well know there is a season for everything, and Shrovetide is the time for the matches. The young man thinking of marrying would go to a spokesman and tell him to visit a particular house in search of a woman for him. The man of that house might have two or three daughters of marriageable age and just ripe for the taking. The spokesman and the young fellow then went off to him together. The spokesmen were glib talkers : if they weren't like that they wouldn't be any good at their job. When they reached the young woman's house the spokesman knocked on the door, and the man of the house would open the door and enquire : "What drove yourself on this road since 'tis rarely you visit us?"—but, at the same time I suppose the man of the house half suspected what brought him. The spokesman would give the stick in his fist a shake and say : "I came seeking one of your daughters for this particular man," as he named the young fellow. "Come in and sit down 'till we have a talk a while," was the answer.

'After entering the first thing the spokesman would do was to take out an old bottle he had in his pocket and give a glass out of the bottle to the man of the house in the hope that it might soften him. He then started to praise the youth to the very skies : his mode of life, his stock, his worldly substance, leaving not a

106

single stone unturned so that he couldn't be refused. After the father had a brief conversation with his daughter it wouldn't take him long to give him a promise. The spokesman would then ask : "What dowry will you be able to give with this girl?" "I'll do my best; I'll give you the amount my means will allow me to give her." The bargain would be struck and the match made.

'When all the negotiations were over that was the time the young man came in, and the father would say : "We had better get some drink and invite the relations"—for it was only close relations and next-door neighbours who used to be invited to a matchmaking party. They brought back a half-tierce of stout with them for that was the drink at every matchmaking long ago. From then till morning the whole crowd had a grand, merry night.

'First thing in the morning the young lad would go to the curate's house, where he would be given a letter for the parish priest for it was the parish priest who demanded the money for the wedding from them; furthermore if there was any degree of relationship between them they would have to go to see the bishop in order to fix things.

'I myself remember very few Cape Clear couples who married that weren't wed by the parish priest in Ráth church. When they came home that's the time there used to be the great feast with the house full—and dance-music and songs, eating and drinking throughout the night. I suppose that many was the man who had only the memory of the previous late night's festivity as the sole support for his spirit when he was sluggish with sickness after the night's sport!

'Another thing to remember is that matches were arranged only on a Sunday, Tuesday or Thursday night, and also that the newly-married woman who didn't change to her new home before Shrove was past had to stay until Easter. Whether she went in Shrovetide or at Easter, the night the young woman had fixed on to move, her husband and a small group would come to meet her on the road. In the same way there would be an equally small number of the wife's relatives setting out to accompany her to her new home. When they met the two groups stayed with the young wife, and no sooner was she inside the door than her husband's mother was standing before her in the middle of the floor. She used to take the cloak from the young woman's shoulders—at that time every woman who married wore a cloak. After that she took her by the two hands and said :

> Wisha, O'Kelly's welcome to you,
> A welcome and forty to you all,
> And may the young pair have seven sons!

'There is neither drinking, nor feasting, nor celebrations at a wedding or matchmaking today, and it's a long time since there was : everything is too costly and people have to spend sparingly in proportion to their purses. And, as ye know, there are no spokesmen to do matchmaking today, but the two thinking about marrying confide in one another, go to the priest and get the job done. That leaves the uninvited scroungers without as much drink as would drown a bee. And that's more of the old ways gone for ever, boys.[6]

'As I said already a change has come over everything in my lifetime. Yes, and I remember when there was no barrel-churn for making the butter. After the cows were milked in the evening the pans were washed clean with boiling water and left to dry in the sun in preparation for the morning's milking. The milk was poured through a strainer into pans both morning and evening, and was left to settle for a while without being stirred. When the time was ripe the cream was skimmed from the milk, and to hold it they had a two-handed crock that was called the "keeler" or the cream-crock. In order to make the butter they used an appliance known as a mether or dash-churn which had a narrow mouth, while the rest of it was broad. It came from the hand of the cooper and was made of boards of oak bound by hoops of iron. Close to the top of the mether's mouth there was a detachable cover with a hole in its centre through which a stick called a churn-dash was inserted. At the base of this was a circular piece of oak, called a plunger, which had five or six holes pierced in it.[7]

'When the time came for churning all the cream was poured into the mether and the dash was put down into the cream before the wooden cover was placed in position with two feet of the handle of the dash protruding from it so that a person could catch it with his two hands and stir it around continuously to break up the cream until the butter was finally made.[8]

'If it were to happen that one of the neighbouring women came in while the churning was being done, the one doing it would say: "Here, take a turn at the churning before you leave." When the neighbour caught hold of the churn-dash with her hands this is what she said:

> God's blessing be on this churning,
> May no straw or dribble be in it,
> And may there be no more hairs in it
> Than there are thick pounds of butter!

It was said that if the person who came in didn't take a turn at the churning before leaving there would be a risk that she would take the worth of the butter on her road with her, and that no churning would make the butter.'

'How would she take the butter with her in that way?' asked Donnchadh.

'Wisha, my dear friend, may we suffer no more harm than what comes from merely knowing about it![9] You know well that there's nothing in the whole business except pishogues and, as I have heard, they were very plentiful in the old days.'

CHAPTER FOURTEEN

*How the people of Cape Clear asserted
their rights against their earthly lord.*

'Cape Clear is beyond the law.'[1] So goes a proverb we have here among ourselves. The Island is cut off from the mainland of the south-west of Ireland and lies out in the Atlantic and, as a bad result of that, certain matters were in a proper tangle throughout the mainland long before news or tidings of them reached the Island.

When the old folk here heard talk of the Land League and the reports that came from the land outside that the farmers of the country were going into court against their landlords to get a reduction in their rents, their very hearts used to change colour to think that any tenant had the courage to go to law with his earthly lord. They didn't believe it any more than they would credit that you could walk on the sea.

On a Sunday morning the priest spoke from the altar and said : 'Let ye all be at Tra Ineer near my house at two o'clock, for a boat from the mainland will have arrived there at that time. A man will come over to Cape Clear in her this evening to tell ye something which will be of benefit to ye, and I hope that ye won't forget to be at the meeting.'

It was a fine autumn evening. When the boat was seen approaching the harbour the person who would wait to put on his stockings wouldn't wait to put on his shoes, through the dint of his hurry to get to the meeting, for it was the first public meeting ever held in the Island.

When they were all present together they hadn't long to wait until the man who was to present his argument came among them. He stood up on the ditch and began to speak, and you may well say that he was a great hand at it : he had the most fluent tongue of Irish I ever heard.

This is what he said : 'Friends and fellow countrymen, I hear that you are still in bondage to the landlord; but if you act as I will tell you to you won't be long so. Do what your neighbours over there across the water have done : keep the rent back from the landlord; go into court against him and I give you my word and my hand that you will get satisfaction from him as good as any group of people did in the mainland. It is you people who have the real opportunity to do it. There isn't any section of the people from the Giants' Causeway in the north of Ireland to the lonely island of Cape Clear better able to obtain their due rights than yourselves. And I'll tell you why: if you were evicted from your patches of land tomorrow you have the boats to live in—something that many more haven't got at all; and I assure you that no one would have the gall to take over his fellow-creature's patch of land.'

They all agreed with him and promised that they would be loyal and steadfast in the campaign. He then told them that the priest would be their leader and he added, 'I'll do my best, and I'll give you all the help and advice I am able to.' That evening every tenant on the Island received a card of membership which stated that he would play his part in the movement and be loyal in defending the rights of all against the landlord.

When the time came to pay the rent nobody did so. When the second gale day came it wasn't paid either. Still nobody was evicted from his house, nor was there any talk of it. The next news they heard was that a land-valuer was coming into the Island to value the land, and when he arrived he went from end to end of the Island and into every single farm.

I remember rightly the day he came to see our place. After taking a walk through the farm, such as it was he sat down at the foot of a ditch and began to do some writing on a map he had. I heard my father saying to him: 'That rough trashy ground isn't worth much.'

The answer he gave him was: 'Ah my good fellow, a cow can't walk without bones.'

'Indeed,' said my father promptly, 'the cow without flesh on its bones isn't of much value.'

From day to day after that everyone was waiting for and anticipating the day for the court, for the Land Court was naturally on everyone's lips. When any two of the old men met one would say to the other: 'Who could imagine that a time would ever come that a poor "angishore" like me or yourself would be able to go to court quite freely and independently against our earthly lord.'

111

'I hope we will have cause to laugh, man,' his companion would say, 'it's certainly a big change in the world. A report came yesterday in the boat returning from the fair outside on the mainland that the majority of the tenants of Ireland were after getting great satisfaction from them.'

'I would think,' the other man would say in reply, 'that the people of Cape Clear should rightly get a greater reduction than would the person who is convenient to the market or a fair.'

'You're right there : an Island shouldn't be compared with the mainland. Look at it like this, man : it is often you saw— and I too—a fellow going to the fair with a beast. He would have to get a boat and crew to bring the beast out the day beforehand. When he and his animal had the freedom of their feet on the mainland, the boat would turn back home and he would drive his beast into the town. He might know someone there that he could make bold on and who would let it into his barn until morning. He would drive his beast to the fair in the morning and whether prices were good or bad he would have to be satisfied and sell it. It is often a Cape Clear man sold his beast for next to nothing when he would be willing to drive it home again if he had dry land under his feet.'

That is the manner in which people used to be deliberating and arguing during the time until the court day came. The priest was their leader so as to give them directions about everything they had to do. He gave them all instructions to go out and pay the attorney between them, and he said that he himself would accompany them and give them all the help and assistance he could.

The day came. The case was called. They all got good satisfaction. Everyone was granted a rebate of a third of his rent, that is six or seven shillings in the pound, on condition that he gave a guarantee that he would be content with that settlement for fifteen years.

When the fifteen years were up—and they longed for those years to pass—they tried once more; but they didn't do as well as they did the first time : they only got a cut of three or four shillings in the pound. Everyone was paying about half of the original rack-rent from then on until we got our own law in the end.[2]

112

Considering what I have told you of the whole story, the young generation there today don't know anything at all about the hard life I and my like had when we were young. When I hear them finding fault with life today I don't say a word to them, but I think to myself in my own mind, ambasa, that if I had such a life when I was young I would consider myself to be king of Ireland. Our small patches of land that we used to pay almost their weight in gold for long ago, they are ours now entirely at our own will with only a mere pittance to be paid for them. We thought at that time that we wouldn't have any thing in the world to complain about again for ever more if things remained as they were. But after the people of Ireland had wrung their rights from the landlords as they pleased even that itself didn't satisfy them; by the Lord they turned to fighting for their cause again and kept at it ably until they got the upper hand of the English once again. We have our own law and government now, and we thank God for the change for the better that has come about. But those who are young today want more. I suppose matters will always be the same : the thing that would satisfy the old man won't please the young one. But, as for myself, I won't have hand, act or part in any other struggle again for I am too old for it, and I suppose I won't be alive for it anyway. Yet my heart and my mind are always on the side of the Irish, and will be as long as I have a breath of life in me, and I pray that they may have success, joy and the grace of God. May God prosper them—although I won't be there or tidings of me.

> Sway and plenty we will have in our country,
> Mansions with high walls will be utterly empty,
> Ireland unchained will be ours alone
> As the beautiful milking maid said.

CHAPTER FIFTEEN

The new quay. The story of the grey water.

Thirty-five years ago there was no harbour in Cape Clear where they could keep their boats in the winter; and in all earnest the value of the boats, nets, and every sort of fishing gear owned by the people of the Island was considerable. They had to keep their boats in safe harbours on the mainland to protect them, and everyone realises that that didn't suit them but that they would rather have them in their own harbour at home where they could best keep an eye on them.

At that time, naturally, all the Irish Boards—as well as everything else—were under English control and direction. Day after day and from year to year, efforts were being made to do something about a harbour that would convenience the fishermen and enable them to protect their property in their own Island. For a long time, however, a deaf ear was being turned to them.

At length Timothy Sheehy, a good man from Skibbereen, who was troubled by the complaints of the people of the Island, went over to England for the express purpose of doing something about the matter. He was promised a substantial grant of money for the building of a safe harbour in Trakieran. Shortly afterwards a man came from the Board of Works in Dublin to examine and survey the site in order that he might give his opinion of what was to be done and how best to use the money.

After he had gone back the work started, and it lasted three years without a break from the day it began until it was finished. The job was completed most satisfactorily : inside the quays a dock was constructed so that, when the boom-gate was closed, a cable from a boat was no better than a little thread of wool for mooring her—however stormy the weather.[1]

The year the work began almost all those engaged in it were strangers from outside the Island; the men of the Island wouldn't give up the fishing for any other job for it was of that they had the greatest experience. But that year the fishing season was a failure : after clearing their expenses they had very little left. When Christmas was past a lot of the fishermen went to work on the dock for the strangers left their jobs : it was so

114

expensive for them on the small wages that they had nothing left over after their time, and so they went home.

I myself stayed working there the whole time until the beginning of the following spring. But when the potatoes were set that meant the start of the fishing season.

One morning after my breakfast a boy came in the door to me and said : 'My father sent me to call on you to go fishing because they are short a man.'

I pondered on the matter for a while before I gave him my answer for, to tell the truth, I intended to go working on the dock again.

'By the Lord Himself,' I replied, 'I won't refuse you; I'll go along with ye.'

When I got as far as the quay I met the boss : 'You are up to something,' he said when he saw my makeshift bed on my shoulders.

'Do you know what you'll do now,' he continued; 'don't bother about your fishing but come back to work here and I'll give you six shillings a day from this until the work is finished.' I suppose he was tempting me to be greedy for that was double pay.

'I won't,' I said; 'whatever I would get from you I won't stay on the job, for a man must keep his word, and since I promised this particular man that I'd go fishing with him I won't go back on my word and make a lie of it.'

It has ever been said that what a person thinks the worst thing in the world turns out to be something to his profit. We left the harbour the same evening and fished for that night; we got a fair catch of fish and so went to the fish-market in Baltimore on the following day. We anchored in the harbour and the captain said : 'Put the tackle in the punt, lads, and launch her so that I can go ashore in search of some small things I need.'

The cook and he pulled for the shore. A short while after we noticed the boat connected with the work in Cape Clear passing by us with six men at the oars in her and a man at the helm. We didn't pay any special attention to her for the same boat used often be ferrying between Cape Clear and Baltimore.

When our captain returned he said : 'Conchúr, do you know what?' 'I don't then,' I answered.

'Well,' said he, 'you were the fortunate man that you didn't go to work on the job that time yesterday.'

'Why so?' I asked.

'Well,' he said, 'they were shifting a load yesterday evening with that crane on the new quay and the stays gave so that it toppled over the quay-side carrying the men working nearby. Nothing happened to anyone except only to the engineer; he has a big gash in his head. Bringing him to the doctor they were that time.'

'It has ever been said,' I remarked, 'that accidents are always possible, if only one could avoid them.'

Upon my word it was a great pity because it was easy to work for him : he wasn't sour, or abusive, or given to spying on the men from afar; still the work was done just as well as if he was always bawling at them. I myself gave the whole year working for him and I never saw any sign of dissatisfaction on him except for one night only. Some of us had to do tidal work, and we were due to go to work this particular night at ten o'clock. He arrived on the site when it was time, looked about him, and asked where the foreman was. Naturally nobody answered him although we knew well where he was. He became angry and went looking for him. He found him asleep in the forge; yet he didn't disturb him but left him where he was and came back to the men again.

When we went to work in the morning, however, we were surprised that the foreman wasn't there to give us directions about the work. The boss himself it was who came along to us in his stead. It wasn't long until we saw poor Seán—for that was the foreman's name—coming along the strand making for the mail-boat carrying his traps and his gear, and he off home. That is what he earned for his sleep in the forge. It has always been said that the doorsteps to the Big Houses are slippy, and so a man with ambition should attend to the responsibilities of his job.

When we realised what was after happening every single one of us drove the point of whatever tool he had in his hand into the ground. 'What are ye up to now?' said the boss.

One of the workmen spoke out quite independently and said up to his very face that we were going on strike unless he would

116

call that man back. He went off at once, and before Seán managed to board the mail-boat he intercepted him and called him back. 'It is my opinion,' he said, 'that these men here have a high opinion of you, and so you can return to your work again.'

That shows you that to be united is to be able to resist the power of authority.

After giving up the job on the quay I stuck to the fishing, and I can tell you that it is fishermen and seamen who encounter strange experiences.

I recall—and I have good reason to remember it well—that we left the harbour on a Monday morning after taking a week's supply of water with us as was usual. Fishermen show more interest in and are fonder of the fresh water than they worry about even their food. They have to see to it that no one uses it excessively or wastefully. If it were to happen that one of the men rubbed a drop on his face to wash himself another would say : 'If you are going to the fair it would be fitter for you to put on a collar and cravat, give your boots a rub of a brush, and wipe the fish scales off them !'

Fish were scarce that week, and when catches were light as I am saying, the boats used to spread out and move away from one another in order to search for them on their own.

On the Thursday morning of that particular week we let the boat sail on a course directly south, until we were forty miles from land, in the hope and expectation that fish could be caught there, for old fishermen used to say that in the month of May mackerel made for the open sea. The evening was calm and clear and we shot our nets there; and when we had everything in order and had the boat headed into the wind the cook was ordered to put the kettle on the fire so that we could have our supper. The first word of reply we heard from him was that there was a hole in the cask and that there wasn't a drop of water left. The cook was right : it was empty. That increased our thirst more than ever for we were after eating our fill of fish the previous evening, and although it was fresh fish there is nothing one can eat that makes one thirstier than fish, especially when it is boiled in salt water—and on a boat fish was always prepared in that way.

It couldn't be helped; we had to make the best of it; suffer and be patient.

'Let us ask for the grace and mercy of God, boys,' said the captain, 'what we must do is haul the nets as quickly as possible and start shortening the way to the land as long as we have a fair breeze with us.'

But, as the saying has it, 'the ship doesn't make the point on the shore that it is headed for.' We set out to work straightaway and we had the nets on board by the time the dawn broke. But instead of the breeze's getting stronger it was the way it died away entirely; and when the sun rose the water was dead-calm and lustrous so that a boat wouldn't stir even if she had a hundred sails no her.

We didn't know then what we should do. We couldn't think of anything else but of when help would come to us which would quench our thirst. 'Diarmuid,' said the captain to one of the boys, 'since you have the youth and the light heart climb up the mast to see if you can catch a glimpse of any boat or vessel at all'

No sooner was the word out of his mouth than the young man clambered up the rigging and in the twinkling of an eye he was standing on the mast-end of the gaff with his arm around the mast.

I called out a question from below : 'Do you see anything?'

'By the Lord I do,' he replied; 'a big four-masted ship away out there,' and he pointed out the direction with his hand.

'Is she far from us?'

'No,' he answered; 'by right ye should be able to see her from the deck.' That very moment we all saw her.

'Well, boys,' said the captain, 'the ear is no closer to the head than God's help is to the body. Lower the punt and let three of you go in her with the keg and row out to the ship to see if ye can get some water from him. And don't forget to bring him a meal of fresh fish.'

Three of us jumped aboard the punt and the keg and fish were thrown down to us. We pushed off from the side, two of us rowing and one steering, and because of the ship's appearing to be so big we thought before we left our boat that she was no more than two miles from us. But it wasn't so. It took us more than an hour before we reached her as we rowed our best on a broiling hot day. You can well say that there was sweat in our boots by that time.

She was like an island in the middle of the ocean with not a puff of wind blowing that would stir her. She had four masts which were covered with gleaming sails that were as white as snow. The hull itself was painted from the water-line up.

We were no sooner alongside than one of the sailors threw down the end of a rope to us. A ladder was then lowered and two of us went on board. The captain was striding up and down on the quarter-deck astern, and we went for'ard to talk to him and to explain our predicament : how we hadn't a single drop of water from the previous evening and would be very thankful to him if he could give us any amount he had to spare.

'You can have it,' he said; 'I will give you the sort I have and you are welcome to it. It is up to two years since we left England and went to India. There we got a cargo for Australia, and now we have a ship-load of wheat from Australia for England. That is a long voyage,' he said, 'but we still have on board some of the same water that we loaded in England, and you will get your keg-full of it.'

The keg was passed up from the punt and also the strop of fresh fish When the captain saw the fresh fish he was delighted beyond bounds and called his wife out of the cabin to see it; and however well it pleased himself I can tell you that it gave her far greater pleasure.

He ordered one of the sailors to fill the keg with water for us and the sailor put it under a pump by means of which he drew water from the bottom of the ship. When we saw the colour of the water we looked at it in bewilderment : it seemed more like milk than water for it had a sort of strange pale white colour.

'Don't be a bit surprised at the colour the water has,' he said. 'Any water that spends a long spell stagnant in a container changes its colour, but bit by bit the colour will alter again until it will be as clear as the day it left the well. However, I must warn you about one thing,' he added, 'don't drink it like that without boiling it. We use it on board from time to time, but when there is rainy weather we save the water that drips from

119

the canvas by putting vessels under it.'

While we were preparing to leave the captain told us to wait until he returned from his quarters. There was scarcely a minute's delay before he came back with two bottles and a glass, and he gave each of us a glass of spirits to drink from one of the bottles. 'That will give you heart for the long row you have before you,' he said, 'and here's a bottle of rum for you to bring to your shipmates. On your life don't taste a drop of it until you are aboard your own boat.'

He also gave us a pound of tea. 'That,' he said, 'comes to you just as it was picked in the fields and there is no need to put much of it in the water. I'm sorry that I can't do better for you, but we had a long voyage and our stores are practically exhausted, almost as if a woman was down to her last hairpin.' We thanked him and wished him every good fortune in wind and weather until he reached his journey's end—and then we left.

It didn't take us too long to reach our boat for the drop of spirits had indeed given us zest for rowing. While we were coming alongside we were asked if we had anything for them.

'We have,' I answered : 'two things—in fact three : a keg of water, a bottle of rum full to the brim, and a pound of tea just as it left the plant.'

'Musha,' they called out to us, 'you're welcome yourselves, and what you bring with you is welcome !'

We told them what instructions we got about the water, that we were to boil it and not drink it as it was. 'By the Lord, wisha,' said one of the crew, 'I couldn't have patience to wait until it is boiled. I'll take a drink of it as it is whatever it will do to me.' He swallowed a basinfull of it and it did him no harm.

When the kettle was boiled we put in some of the tea to try it, but we noticed that the water still retained the same colour. I couldn't deny that everyone tasted it; but it was no more than that, for we couldn't bring ourselves to drink it even though we were in dire need of it.

Then, when the sun was at its highest, the light breeze strengthened, for it was 'sea-turn' weather when the wind follows the sun's course, and it is usual that a good breeze of

120

wind blows at that time of the day; and as the sun begins its long descent the wind starts to lighten until it dies away with the coming of night.[2] We hoisted the sails and put her head towards the land. We were running full enough, a couple of points from the wind and carrying a few feet of sheet, trimming our sail to suit the wind—our bend being drawn through the water with the dip of the sail. I can tell you that she was making grand way at that time.

After we had made about twenty miles way we saw a barque on a broad reach from the east because of the wind. Ourselves and this vessel were set on courses that would cause us to cross one another as he beat into the wind and we ran with it. We held our course, and came up under his stern and hailed him. He was asked if he would be able to give us a keg of water, and he said that he could, and told us to launch our punt. She was put into the water straightaway and two of us jumped into her. We didn't forget to bring a feed of mackerel with us for our man, and what we got from him was a keg-full of grand, pure, fresh water—and this time we all quenched our thirst in earnest.

When this water was boiled it was the tea from the big ship that was put into it. Wasn't it we were amazed that our tea didn't colour the water as it should rightly do! But still it was as fine, as tasty, and as delightful to drink as any tea I ever drank.

CHAPTER SIXTEEN

The fisherman's life during the First World War. The reason why the fishing failed.

Before the war began fish were few and far between, and after meeting their expenses fishermen had little to show at the end of the season for all their work. We used to say among ourselves that it was the English trawlers that were responsible for the fish being wiped out.

But as soon as the war began England called all her trawlers home and they got a different type of fishing job to do. They were sent out to defend the coast, and watch out for the enemy, here, there, and everywhere along its whole extent.

They had no sooner been summoned home than the fish crowded in towards the coast in more profusion that I ever remembered before that : all we had to do was to go out for them and catch all we could take in the boats every single night. But however plentiful they were the demand for them yonder in England was so great that it wasn't possible to keep them supplied with enough—for they had nothing to show of their own as far as fish were concerned.[1] The fishermen could then get full value for a fine fish just as the farmer could for his own stock; 'a golden tail on a pig and a hornful of gold on a cow' was a saying we used then. And I can tell you that whatever shape they were in little fault was found with them, and there was no talk of 'foot and mouth disease', although the cattle used to have it everyday before then—if one was to believe the people across the water.

But I'm talking about fishermen : when they were out fishing they were right in the very centre of the war day and night, with the air-ships above them that no one knew where they were going to or coming from, and below them the submarines that couldn't be seen until one of them popped up to the surface alongside the boat without one's knowing whether they were foes or friends, and, far more hazardous and menacing still than those, the mines, that one couldn't see at all, fixed as they were between two waters and full of menace. When one considers all those things that were lying in wait for a man I can assure you that it was truly enough to make an old man out of any young one who was trying to earn his living in the midst of fire and water.

It was terrible entirely in foggy weather. I recall one such time when we had shot our nets. During the night we used to hear a strange sound that we couldn't find any cause for, or even where exactly it was located. From time to time something peculiar happened below us that caused a disturbance on the surface of the water which rocked our boat badly and shook her from stem to stern. And during every one of these occasions you would swear on the Book that it was how old buckets were being hauled through the water and were grating and scraping roughly against one another under the keel. We said to one another that it was probably a fleet of submarines that was there because nothing else could cause such noise.

That was surely a terrifying time to be at sea. Very few days passed that some damage wasn't done after the night, with a ship or steamer sunk and sometimes corpses strewn about the water just as you would see the rods of *loke* seaweed on a strand. The fishing boats that came across the drowned brought them into the harbour and handed them over to the officials. Many are the corpses from foreign parts that are buried around the coast of Ireland.

The fishermen were getting off scot-free for a long time without any harm happening to either themselves or their craft. But the 'crúiskeen' that is constantly going to the well is broken in the end.

One Monday night all the boats set out from the harbours wherever they happened to be. The Cape Clear boats chanced to be on the western end of the fleet and the boats from other places stretched away in a line eastwards from them. When all the boats had shot their nets and had their stems to the sea, a German came up unexpectedly to the surface at the eastern end of the fleet, just as a cat would jump at a mouse the moment he was least expecting it. He headed for the closest boat and said: 'Launch your punt and go aboard that boat nearest to you for I am about to sink your boat.' Naturally it seemed an eternity to them until they had fled for their lives. It wasn't long until the big fishing boat was at the bottom of the sea.

He handed out the same treatment to a great number of boats that same night but he let all the men go free. Eventually he came across a small undecked boat that had no punt on board and gave them the same order : to go aboard the boat that he had ordered the others into a while perviously, and let their own boat go with the sea. The German then drew away but instead of doing as he was commanded what did the captain of the small boat do but make for the patrol boat that was in close to the shore, for he knew where to head in order to find her. When he reached him he told him that the German was outside in the middle of the fleet sinking the boats as fast as he could. The men of the patrol boat proved their mettle for they went out to hunt for the German, and just like the rabbit that would go into its burrow from a dog when he saw it the German disappeared under the water at once and so closed the door behind him. But for that happening all but a few of the fishing boats would have been sunk by morning.

Thanks be to God the Cape boats came out of it all well; neither a man nor a boat suffered any harm or hurt from the German. What caused that but that he didn't get as far west as they happened to be when he had to beat a rapid retreat.

Throughout the war the Cape men continued to argue about the pros and cons of things, but they couldn't stop fishing; they were obliged to risk their lives constantly in order to feed themselves and their families at home. They earned a lot of money without any doubt in the world but, if they did everything was so dear and costly that there were great calls entirely on their earnings : it was nothing but 'here it is for you! Show me your money!'—their money melted away utterly as quickly as it was earned.

Although the people of Cape Clear came out of things well during the war misfortune overtook them at last when they were least expecting it. I'll tell you how.

One day I was cutting a back-load of furze. It was in the month of November after the war was over. When I had secured my handful of furze with a rope I stood still for a moment and looked back west at the bay. I noticed a very small boat leaving the harbour with three men in her, two rowing and one steering. I examined the scene more intently and spotted a big, black bulky lump towards which the boat was pulling.

It wasn't long afterwards until a second boat—a motor yawl —came out of the harbour with five men in her. Quite naturally it passed out the rowing boat, because of its speed, and was heading for the lump which was floating in with the tide from the west.

What should it be but a mine and it wasn't long making itself known. The moment the yawl brushed against it, it exploded. I often heard a loud peal of thunder but I never heard such a crack of sound as that thing made the time it exploded. A pall of smoke that was blacker than tar rose from it. The sky and the sea round about became jet-black, so dark that I couldn't see a thing for a few minutes.

I thought to myself that no one in either boat could have survived, and that I wouldn't be able to give them any other help than by saying a prayer for them at that time. I recited the Act of Love and Contrition two or three times as fervently as I ever said it.

But when the smoke scattered and when everything could be seen clearly, I noticed that the small boat had survived; but there was neither sign nor presence, trace nor tidings of the yawl to be seen : matchwood had been made of her in an instant. Four of the men were lost; the blessing of God on their souls, and may He preserve all those where the story is told ! The one who could see the horror that occurred that day would say that if a whole parish of people were there not a single one would escape alive; but yet the fifth man did. No harm was done to the small boat nor to anyone of those in her. They lifted the survivor on board and searched the place for the other men. They came across one only, and they brought his body ashore.

You can well say that this was the sad sorrowful evening in Cape Clear. It has always been said that the worst of all livings is that won from the sea.

Returning to the fishing again, every sort of fish was as plentiful at that time as it could be; but as soon as the trawlers went to work again the fish turned their backs on the coast so that they are scarcer this very day than they were at any time I can remember. If it goes on like that the young people who are growing up to the age of manhood won't be able to distinguish between a ling and a hake, or a cod and a haddock; they won't know how they should put bait on a hook or how they should prepare a line for fishing. That is something they can't be blamed for : no one understands a job he has never seen. The saying of the wise men long ago was—

> Until the crab would abandon the sea,
> And fish would leave harbour and estuary
> And until the friend would fail his fellow.

Those are great wonders; but I would consider it as great a miracle if such a change were to come in the world as would cause the men of Cape Clear to abandon the fishing.

CHAPTER SEVENTEEN

Winding in the line and making an end.[1]

On a Saturday, in or about forty years ago, I was ashore in Baltimore. I went into a public house to drink as it is usual that fishermen are utterly parched with the thirst after the week's fishing. It happened that there was a stranger there seated on the same bench beside me. I was astonished when he spoke Irish to me that I noticed was different from the Irish I had. One thing I recall clearly was that he called a *capall* a *cabhall,* and for *coirce* he used the word *sligeach.* But still we were able to chat with one another in the end just as much as we pleased. I asked him where he was from and he said that he came from the Isle of Man and that he was a fisherman from one of the boats out in the harbour. I then asked if the Irish language was being kept up in that place of his, and did everyone there speak it as well as he himself did. 'It isn't wisha,' he said, 'except for a little of it that is spoken in the countryside, but not one word of it is spoken now in village or town.'[2]

I hear that scarcely a word of Irish is being spoken in that place today, and the same thing all but happened among ourselves. What I would compare our situation to is just as if a fire would be out except that a few burning embers still remained in the ashes of the fireplace. That is exactly the way it is with Irish. But it is often I myself said at the time, when the strongest efforts were being made to kill the Irish, that there would be affection and respect for it yet—whoever would live to see it; and that the fire would be kindled again so that it would flame up gradually until it was fully ablaze as glowing and radiant as it was before. Sometimes there was little respect for my view, but ambasa my prophecy came true.

They have devised a lot of ways now to keep the Irish alive. For example they are thinking about taking the people of the *Gaeltacht* from the patches of land they have and settling them in the centre of Ireland. In this way they would have done two beneficial things : the people of the *Gaeltacht* would have fine, smooth, level land instead of the trash they had previously; and the Irish would be being spoken widely among people who didn't have a word of it.[3]

That is a good plan : to give some broadening of their vision to the *Gaeltacht* people which would lift them out of their life of poverty, for they themselves and penury have been struggling with one another long enough. I am positive that there are people in the *Gaeltacht* who will like that scheme, and I wouldn't say a word against them. But certainly, as regards myself, if I were asked tomorrow to leave this wild, harsh place and to go to live where I would have every advantage, convenience, and opportunity I could wish for, this is what I would say : although I have lean cheeks and a stooped back from trying to make a living throughout my life in this isolated place, far from market or fair, still I and the patch of land I own, are so used to one another that I couldn't leave it. And another thing—if I were to go to a place now where I wouldn't have any sight of the sea I am sure that my ration of life would soon be spent. I have been here all my life, and as I have burned the nails' breadth I will burn the inch for I have gone so far now that I will finish my life here. I will stay where I am until my bones are stretched in Killkieran where all my ancestors for seven generations before me are buried.

But there is still another method being devised for reviving the Irish language, and I think a lot of it—if it is really put into effect. The whole world knows that the quicker the young generation are sent to the *Gaeltacht* and the younger they are when Irish is spoken to them that that is the very best thing for them, for when they learn it while they are young there will be no chance of their ever losing it, and they won't find it hard or troublesome to speak it. To prove my point I'll give you a good example of that.

I had a school pal long ago : we were of the one age too. When he was a young man, and capable of fending for himself, he went to America. He settled down well there and made a home and career for himself. After spending forty years of his time there he came back to see his people and his native place, and he didn't forget to come to see me either. The first words out of his mouth as he came in the door to me were a blessing in Irish. I welcomed him and we spent a while talking about old times. 'Well,' I said to him at last, 'I often heard that a man and his characteristics will be enduring in his own district, but no one would imagine from you that you ever left home for you speak Irish as fluently as ever, just as if you never left the Island at all.'

' 'Tis very little of it I spoke,' he said, 'since I went away; but believe me this : as soon as I put my foot on the Island it began to come back to me again.'

And truly I'm not telling a word of a lie; no one would imagine that he spoke any other language—he didn't make a single mistake. That much tells you that the person who learns Irish from his youth will always have it implanted in his mind so that he will be capable of using it when the occasion arises.

They are now planning to send the young people into the *Gaeltacht* so that they may speak to the old people in every part of it. It is a good idea, indeed an excellent one. But a single month there won't be of much benefit; they should be a year among the old people talking and listening to them—just as was the case with me when I was young and used to be chatting with that old man I called Glavin, and others of his kind. That's the thing that would make native speakers of the young folk; after a few years they would be as apt and as fluent speakers as the old people in the *Gaeltacht* this very day.

Everyone knows what the tide is like when it starts to flood. According as the water is rising it is spreading out and spurting into every place so that it doesn't leave a harbour or a strand, an inlet or a rock-crevice, nor any hidden bay, or hole or corner that it doesn't fill. And I think that the tide of Irish is beginning to fill in the self-same way.

But I suppose that I won't be able to do much to help in that matter; however I will do whatever is in my power, whether God leaves me alive for a long or short time. I will not hold back as much as a single word of the ancient heritage of the speech that I inherited from the old people : I wouldn't have such meanness in my mind nor crankiness in my heart at this time of my life as to conceal or cloak anything I ever heard that would be of any benefit in the work. And so I am now doing my best, before the shovels throw the clay over my eyes, to leave that heritage as a legacy to the young that are growing up to take my place.

APPENDIX ON PLACENAMES

Ireland is a land where the past is ever present, both in the minds of men and in the landscape. (Prof. E. Estyn Evans, *Prehistoric and Early Christian Ireland,* London, 1966, p. 1).

Placenames rarely survive the centuries in span-new condition, even where they have remained untarnished by alien influences. It is a small miracle that so many Irish names have come down to us so as to be decipherable, somehow—as if in a palimpsest—beneath the overwriting in centuries of alien rule that distorted and deformed them almost beyond belief.

Considering the difficulties it would be foolhardy of one who is an amateur in the field to do anything more than suggest explanations and indulge in hypotheses that may happily hit their marks on a rare occasion. I am, of course, thinking here of certain Cape Clear names so ancient that they do not readily yield up information about their origins; for the most part the names present no great problems as they have escaped the full impact of the invaders influence.

Three choices were open to me in deciding what to do about the placenames in the text and on the map: firstly, I could leave the pure Irish originals intact and explain them in an appendix; secondly, it was open to me to use direct translations of the originals—where possible; and my third option was to employ approximate 'phonetic' equivalents of the originals and leave elucidation to an appendix. I decided to adopt my third option, although not without some misgivings. This choice is not an ideal solution, but there is more in its favour than could be put forward for the other options. For one thing anglicised forms of most of the names are used in the Ordnance Survey maps, and these are not significantly different from my 'phonetic' transcriptions. Secondly, the exotic tang is retained for those ignorant of Irish—and this I consider important, despite the length or clumsiness of the equivalents.

A SPECIAL NOTE

Collymore and Collybeg

Although these do not appear in their Irish forms in Ó Síocháin's book they cannot be ignored as they are the names of two districts—bordering the river Ilen—which preserve, in a corrupt form, the ancient name of the pre-Godelic *Corca Laidhe* who gave their name to the territory they occupied. A transitional form of the name in Irish was *Cothluidhe,* and this clearly lies behind *Colly-.*

Italian 'portolan' maps of the Middle Ages have *Corcala,* which seems to represent an earlier form of the original than the Irish *Cothluidhe,* as does Korkly which appears in a Statute of King Henry VI of England, dated 1450 (see *Celtic Miscellany* s.va., and p 141f.).

Places Outside Cape Clear and its Immediate Environs

Abbeystrewery: (a) *Mainistir Bhéal na Sruthra* (?). (b) *Mainistir an tSruthair* (=Abbey of the Stream). See *Pococke,* p 133, and Note 7, Chapter 3, and *Sruthair* in O'Donovan's Suppl. to O'Reilly's *Irish-English Dictionary.*

Baltimore: (a) *Baile an Tí Mhóir* (=Town of the Big House), or alternatively, (b) *Dún na Séad* (=Fort of the Jewels). The name of an O'Driscoll castle which taken with the castles *Dún an Óir*—Fort of the Gold—on Cape Clear were three of the major strongholds of the O'Driscoll sept until the disaster of Kinsale, 1602.

Barna an Cleeve: *Beárna an Chlaidhimh* (=Gap of the Sword —a pass or ravine on Mount Gabriel q.v.).

Bólus: *Bolas* or *Ceann Bhóla's,* a promontery in Co. Kerry. The origin of the name is unknown to me.

Cobh: *Cóbh* or *Cóf Chorcaí*=Cove of Cork.

Creagh (prn. **Cree**): *Craoibheach*=Branchy (Place). Trees still abound where the Church of Ireland graveyard and church are situated on the southern branch of the Ilen estuary— a beautiful setting.

Crookhaven: *Cruachán* (=A round hill, shaped like a haycock) is a fishing port and holiday resort on the Cork coast about ten sea miles from Cape Clear.

Castlehaven: *Baile an Chaisleáin* (=Town of the Castle). The reference is to the most easterly of the O'Driscoll castles. The place was important during the aftermath of the Battle of Kinsale. See 'The Life and Times of Bishop Dónal O'Driscoll', Rev. J. Coombes, *J.C.H.A.S.,* 70, 1965, 108-119.

Galley Head: *Dún Déide.* The second element may stand for 'dTéite', the 'd' eclipsis is consequent on the fact that 'Dún' was neutral in Old Irish. Diarmuid Ó Murchú, an expert in place-name origins, suggested to me that the 'Téite' may be related to 'Téite', a woman's name which appears in the famous medieval collection called *Acallamh na Seanórach* and elsewhere in early sources.

Giant's Causeway: *Cúirt an Aithigh* (=Court of the Subterranean Giant). The more usual Irish form of the name is *Clochán na bhFomórach* (='Causeway of the Fomorians' —the latter being legendary-invaders of Ireland).

Glencar: *Gleann Chárthaí* in Co. Kerry (=Glen of Carthy).

Isle of Man: *Oileán Mhanainn* or, better, *Oileán Mhanannáin,* that is 'Island of Manannan' the son of Lear, god of the sea in Irish mythology.

Iveragh: *Uíbh Ráthach,* an ancient territorial region in the extreme south-west of Kerry whose chiefs were the O'Sheas.

Kaynafeölah: *Cé na Feola,* lit. 'Quay of the Meat'. I don't know how this place on the Ilen got its name.

Kedge Island (Smts. **The Kedge**): *Oileán Dhúnlaing* (=The Island of Darling, Dooley or Doolin). These are the anglicised forms of the Irish name *Dúnlaing* for which see index to the *Celtic Miscellany*. See Chapter 10, Note 3, and *Toe Head* in this Appendix.

Kinsale: *Ceann Sáile* (=Head of the (Salt) Sea). If subsequent history means anything one of the decisive battles of the world was fought here in 1601. This catastrophe for the Irish people brought about the ruin of the Irish aristocracy, opened the floodgates to centuries of merciless colonial repression, and thus almost broke the will of the nation to survive. Today Kinsale is a popular holiday resort, especially for lovers of sailing and deep-sea fishing. Its museum shows that the past is not forgotten just as its streets bear a Spanish character as if to remind us of the days Don Aquila spent there.

Loch Hyne: *Loch Aidhne* smts. *Loch Éidhnigh* are the usual Irish forms of the name of this marine, or salt coastal lake. I have come across no explanations of their meanings which are convincing.
Perhaps *Loch Oighinn*=The Pan (-like) Lake—a name which fits its physical setting—might be worthy of consideration.

MacGillacuddy's Reeks: *Cruacha Dubha Ghiolla Coda.* The famous mountains in Kerry which add so much to the splendour of the Lakes of Killarney.

Mount Gabriel: *Cnoc Fhosta* (Hill of the Encampment). Beyond that I can say nothing about the names of this mountain on the mainland north of Cape Clear.

Old Court: *Seana Chúirt.* The remains of an O'Driscoll castle are still to be seen there.

Poulanine: *Poll an Oighinn*=the name of a lake on Mount Gabriel which translated means the 'Hole of the Pan', i.e. the hole in the mountain which is pan-like in formation and contains a lake.

Rath: *Ráth* in Irish too. With Sherkin and Cape Clear islands this district east of Baltimore—and including the village—forms a separate parish.

Roaring Water Bay: *Loch Treasna*=Lake across or ? Peevish Lake.

Schull: *Scoil Mhuire*=St Mary's School—a fishing and tourist resort on the coast north of Cape Clear and at the foot of Mount Gabriel.

Sherkin Island: *Inis Arcáin* or *Orcáin*=Island of the Boar. Compare *Innse hOrc* (=Islands of the Boars). This Celtic name was modified by Viking folk-etymology so that it became the Scandinavian *Orkneyjar* (=Islands of the Young Seals) the modern *Orkney Islands.*

Stags or Stacks, The: *Stácaí na Tuaithe* (=The Stack-shaped Rocks of the District). Cf. *Ceann Tuaithe* (corrupted to 'Toe Head') which is close by. A *tuath,* small as it was, was ruled by a king.

Skibbereen: *An Sciobairín.* (The name is perhaps to be derived from that of some sea-going craft. In early days hundreds of small vessels sailed up the Ilen river to this famous West Cork town.) The place was also called *Gort na Cloiche,* that is 'The Tilled Field of Stone'—a 'gallawn' perhaps. A settler strove to change the town's name to 'Stapletown' in the eighteenth century, but the title did not take.

See *sgibh, sgib*=a ship, in *An Irish-English Dictionary,* E. O'Reilly, Dublin, n.d.

Toe Head: *Ceann Tuaithe*=Headland of District. Here, as in *Stácaí na Tuaithe* (=Stags), the word *tuath* means a 'district occupied by a population-group'. The one in question was *Tuath Rois* (*Tuath Indolaigh*) n. Roscarbery, Co. Cork. See *O.G.,* p 652, and entry for *Kedge Island.*

THE PLACENAMES OF CAPE CLEAR

TOWNLANDS

Ardgort: *An tArdgort*=The High Field.

Ballyieragh North: *Baile Iarthach Thuaidh*=West Townland, North.

Ballyieragh South: *Baile Iarthach Theas*=West Townland, South.

Carhoona: *Ceathrúna*=Quarters, that is a townland comprised of allotments of a quarter of an acre. These were occupied by the poorest of the Island people. The name 'Quarters' is also found in Sherkin Island.

Comillane: *Comaileán* (? *Cúm an Oileáin*=Hollow place or coomb of the island).

Croha East: *Crathach Thoir*=Boggy or marshy place, East.

Croha West: *Crathach Thiar*=Boggy or marshy place, West.

Glenierach: *Gleann Iarthach*=Western Geln.

Glenirach: *Gleann Oirtheach*=Eastern Glen.

Glenmahnuch: *Gleann Meánach*=Middle Glen.

Gortnalour: *Gort na Lobhar*=Field of the Lepers or Sick People.

Keenleen: *Coinlín*=Stubbly Place.

Killickaforavane: *Cill Leice Forabháin*=Churchyard of the Tombstone of Forabhán. Forabhán may be a corruption of Eireamhán, an ancient O'Driscoll first name which still survives.

Knockaunankweehig: *Cnocán an Chaoithigh*='Hillock of the Stranger or Foreigner' or 'Hillock of O'Cowhig', an anglicised form of Cobhthach, a *Corcu Laidhe* name.

Knockaunnamaurnach: *Cnocán na mBáirneach*=Hillock of the Limpets. Limpets were used as a fertiliser.

Lissomona: *Lios Ó Móine*=Ring-fort of 'Ó Móine'. Cf. Ros Ó gCairbre, Rinn Ó gCuanach, and Mainistir Ó dTorna. I cannot explain Ó Móine except to say that it might be a distorted form of Mughain, a saintly woman whose name appears to be preserved in Killimoone, a townland in Sherkin Island. See *Celtic Miscellany,* s.v. in Index.

Other Inland Placenames of Cape Clear

Carrigeenanillir: *Carraigín an Fhiolair*=Little Rock of the Eagle.

Conaire: *Bóthar na Conaireach,* lit.=Road of the Defile.

Coomnakille: *Cúm na Cille*=Coomb or Hollow of the Church or Churchyard.

Cummer: *Cumar*=Ravine, Valley, or Dale.

False Men, The: *Na Fir Bréagacha.* The English name is a literal translation of the Irish. See Note 7, Chapter 10.

Glensmole: *Gleann Smóil*=Thrush Glen.

Killvroon: *Cill Bhrún*=Burial place or Churchyard of Brún. Who Brún was is not clear; but there is evidence for the belief that the place was a pagan cemetery.

Knockeenantowick: *Cnoicín an tSeabhaic*=Small Hill of the Hawk.

Knockfoilandirk: *Cnoc Phoill an Duirc.* Perhaps 'an Duirc' is a corruption of 'Ua Duirc' which appears in the *Corca Laidhe* Genealogy. The meaning would then be The Hill of the Cliff of the Dark or Durk sept. 'Dark' and 'Durk' are anglicised forms of the name. See *Pouladirk,* however.

Lackavuar: *Leaca Mhór*=The Big Hill Slope, a steep road leading east from *Trakieran* q.v.

Loch Ioral: *Loch Ioral.* For this name of the lake in the west of the Island see Note 1, Chapter 11.

Quarantine Hill, Knockcuranteen: *Cnoc Coraintín.* See Note 1, Chapter 10.

Slieve Ard: *An Sliabh Ard*=The High Hill.

Tubbernakille: *Tobar na Cille*=The Well of the Cemetery. This well is linked with *Killbroon* q.v. Significantly it is not regarded as a holy well.

Coastal Placenames of Cape Clear

Ardacushlaun Cliff: *Faill Ard an Chaisleáin*=Cliff of the Height of the Castle, that is Doonanore Castle.

Ardatroha Point: *Pointe Ard an tSrotha*='Point of the Height of the Stream' or, more likely, 'The Current'—a reference, perhaps, to the sea-current at this extreme S.W. headland.

Bawveg: *An Bhá Bheag*=The Small Bay.

Baylnaguyge: *Béal na Gaibhge*=Mouth of the Cleft—through which a streamlet flows from Loch Ioral.

Blánanaragaun: *Bollán na nDeargán.* The Round-shaped Rock of the Bream.

Boilgeen: *An Bhoilgín*=The Little Reef or Concealed Rock.

Bossnaraharsee: *Bas na Raithearsaí. Bas*=anything flat like palm of hand, blade of oar etc. The second element has not yielded up its secret to me.

Bohaunnamnábikte: *Bothán na Mná Boichte*='Cabin of the Poor Woman', whoever she was.

Bollaunnacuniruch: *Bollán na Conaireach*=Round-shaped Rock of the Way or Path.

Carriganayshk: *Carraig an Éisc*=Rock of the Fish (Sg.).

Carraiganclaur: *Carraig an Chláir*=Rock of the Plank or Board.

Carrigancuraun: *Carraig an Chorráin*=Rock of the Reaping Hook or Sickle; perhaps a place where *lóch* was cut to be used as fertiliser.

Carrigancushkame: *Carraig an Choiscéim*=Rock of the Footstep.

Carrigieragh: *An Charraig Iarthach*=The Western Rock.

Carriglee: *An Charraig Liath*=The Grey Rock.

Carriglure: *Carraig Liúir.* See Note 1, Chapter 9, and cf. *An Liúir (Peig,* Peig Sayers, p 210).

Carrignaburtaun: *Carraig na bPortán*=Rock of the Crabs.

Carrignashugee: *Carraig na Seagaí*=Rock of the Shags, or Cormorants.

Carrigeána: *Carraig Éana*=Éanna's Rock. The name Éanna occurs in the *Corca Laidhe* genealogies. See *Miscellany* s.v. in Index. Cf. *Baile Uí Éana, Béal.,* 5, 1935, p 126.

Carrigyleyra: *Carraig Uí Laoghaire*=Rock of O'Leary. I have no information to offer about this O'Leary.

Carrigvuar: *An Charraig Mhór*=The Great Rock, in the Gaiscanaun Sound.

Coolvaw: *Cúlbhá*=Back Bay.

Coolfurtaun: *Cúl Phortáin*=Crab Nook.

Coosancopill: *Cuas an Chapaill*=Cove of the Horse.

Coosadoona: *Cuas an Dúna*=Cove of the Fort. See *Tradoonclayreh.*

Coosadooglish: *Cuas an Dúglais*=Cove of the Black Stream.

Coosangaloonig: *Cuas an Ghallúnaigh*='Cove of the Soap'— association arising perhaps from perpetual foam-flecked sea. According to the Island's folklore this is the spot where the last Englishman in Ireland will be put to death. No Englishman need worry about this.

Coos-angaslawk: *Cuas an Ghasláigh*=Cove of the Green Slimy Weed. The first element is probably a corruption of 'Glas-', and the second a contraction of *-sláthach*=slime. Cf. *salach(ar).*

Coosanglanierig: *Cuas an Ghleanna Iarthaigh*=Cove of the Western Glen.

Coosanishka: *Cuas an Uisce*=Cove of the Water.

Cooslahanaun: *Cuas an Leathanáin*=Cove of the Broad Place or Slope. Cf. *Caolán,* and see *Leahanaun Beg* and *Leahanaun Muar* inf.

Coosanvaud: *Cuas an Bháid*=Cove of the Boat.

Coosduv: *An Cuas Dubh*=The Black Cove.

Coosgurum: *An Cuas Gorm*=The Blue Cove.

Coosheen-Foile-Rónaun: *Cuaisín Faille Rónáin*=The Little Cove of Ronan's Cliff—the name Ronan appears in the *Corca Laidhe* Genealogy (*Celtic Miscellany*, p 37).

Coosheen na Mikehmara: *Cuaisín na Muice Mara*=The Little Cove of the Sea Pig or Porpoise.

Cooslahan: *Cuas Leathan*=Broad Cove.

Coosnaboilge: *Cuas na Boilge*=Cove of the Reef or Concealed Rock.

Coosnagaunogue: *Cuas na gCánóg*=Cove of the Puffins.

Coosanowen: *Cuas an Eoin.* If *Eoin* is not an alternative spelling for *Éin* I have no idea what the last element means. It cannot be the Christian name *Eoghain* (gen.).

Deedaun Beg: *An Díodán Beag.* Unless *Díodán* is an alternative spelling for *Déad-án*=tooth, I find the key word baffling.

Deedaun Muar: See previous note.

Doonanore: *Dún an Óir*=Fort of Gold, the O'Driscoll castle in the Island which Tyrrell surrendered to Sir Roger Harvey in 1602, after the Battle of Kinsale.

Doontomaush: *Dún Tomáis*=Fort of Thomas. I know nothing about this Thomas.

Droumancupoord: *Drom an Chupúird*=The Hump-backed Place of the Cupboard. May have something to do with the shape and general formation of the place.

Foiladda: *An Fhaill Fhada*=The Long Cliff.

Foilanfraykaun: *Faill an Phréacháin*=Cliff of the Crow or Raven.

Foilantarriv: *Faill an Tairbh*=Cliff of the Bull.

Foilard: *An Fhaill Ard*=The Lofty Cliff.

Foilcoo: *Faill Chua.* The second element presents some problems. It can hardly be for *Cuaiche* (gen. sg.) or *'na gCuach'* (gen. pl.). Could it be derived from *Cóch*=a strong gust of wind etc.? Cf. *Slibah gCua* in Waterford (Comeragh Mts.).

Foileekluch: *An Fhaill Fhiaclach*=The Tooth-shaped Cliff.

Foilnabó: *Faill na Bó*=Cliff of the Cow.

Foilnaluinge: *Faill na Loinge (Dóite)*=Cliff of the (Burned) Ship. This name is linked with a sea-battle in which John Paul Jones was engaged. One of the ships set ablaze drifted ashore in Ineer, or Great Harbour.

Foilnalickebwee: *Faill na Lice Buí* = Cliff of the Yellow Slab or Flagstone.

Foilnatayda: *Faill na Téide* = Cliff of the Rope. A rope-walk?

Foilneecahill: *Faill Ní Chathail* = Cliff of Cahill's Daughter.

Foilyearmuda: *Faill Dhiarmada (Chrónacáin)* = Cliff of Diarmaid Crónacáin. The last word is an O'Driscoll soubriquet.

Gaiscanaun: *Gaisceanán.* See *Celtic Miscellany* (p 12ff.) re Amhlaoibh Gascúnach Ó hEidirsceoil, slain by the English at the Battle of Tralee in 1234. From him descended *Clann an Ghascúnaigh.* The suggestion that the name is linked with Gascony is well worthy of consideration.

Garraher: *An Gearathar* = ?The Short Straddle-backed Place. The same placename is attested for a spot in the south-west of Sherkin Island. Could it be that it derives from *Gearr+Srathar* as my tentative translation suggests? It may perhaps come from *Garbh* = rough + *tír* = country, land.

Illaunàhach: *Oileán Athach.* The meaning of the second element is far from clear. The word may be derived from *Fathach* or *Faithche,* that is *Giant* or *Lawn.*

Illaunbeg: *Oileán Beag* = Small Island.

Illaunbrock: *Oileán Broc* = Badger Island.

Illaunéana also **Carrigéana:** *Oileán Éana [Éinne].* An Éanna appears in the *Corca Laidhe* Genealogy. See *Celtic Miscellany,* index.

Illaunnaguard: *Oileán na gCéard* = Island of the Trades or Crafts.

Ineermuar: *Inbhear Mór* = Great Harbour or Estuary, that is South Harbour.

Incerbeg: *Inbhear Beag* = Small Harbour. See map.

Kinrone: *Ceann Róin* = Headland of the Seal.

Lacka Lochaleen: *Leaca Loch an Lín* = Stone Slab of the Flax Pond.

Lacklahard: *Leac Leath-ard* = The Moderately High Slab.

Lekeen: *Leicín* = The Little Flagstone.

Lekeenyihalig: *Leicín Uí Fhicheallaigh* = Little Flagstone of O'Fihelly, a place just west of *Stocaunnaminaun.* The O'Fihellys were a *Corca Laidhe* family and chiefs of *Tuath Ó Ficheallaigh,* an extensive territory n. Baltimore. The most famous member of the sept was Maurice 'de Portu' O'Fihelly, Archbishop of Tuam (1506-1513). He was called 'Flos Mundi' because of his erudition. The *portus* in question is Baltimore.

Ligaunach: *Liogánach*=Liagánach < *Liagán*=pillar-stone, or hand-stone. This placename probably means 'The Stony Place'.

Lugalach: *Logalach* < *Loglach*=a hollow in a cliffside.

Leahanaun Beg; Leahanaun Muar: *Leathanán Beag; Leathanán Mór. Beag*=small; *Mór*=big.

Leathanán is puzzling. 'Leathan'=Broad, large, *fán*=slope. Perhaps the name is compounded from these, which would give *Leathan+fán* > *Leathanán*='the broad or large sloping place or, in this case, cliff'. It may well be made up of *Leath+Fánán* (i.e. half slope or incline).

Lackvwee: *Leac Bhuí*=yellow flagstone.

Oglach Beg; Oglach Lar; Oglach Muar: Three rocks between *Carraig Éana* and the coast of the Island.

Óglach=a vassal, servant, petty chief. The name is used of some *Corca Laidhe* septs as a generic title. See *Celtic Miscellany*. The rock names may have some link with this sense.

Pointantrehin: *Pointe an Treithin.* 'Treathan'=sea, high water. It was originally the gen. sg. of 'triath' (=the sea) in O. Irish.

The name would seem therefore to mean 'sea point' or 'high water point'.

Rare : only two entries in *O.G.*

Pointnaboilge: *Pointe na Boilge*='Point of the submerged reef'.

Pointnapayshte: *Pointe na Péiste*='Point of the serpent or monster'.

Pointnaranarue: *Pointe na Reanna Rua*='Point of the red-coloured headland'.

Pouladirk: *Poll an Duirc. Poll*=a hole. For the rest of the name refer to the note on *Cnoc Phoil an Duirc.* J. O'Donovan's Suppl. to O'Reilly *Irish-English Dict.* however has *dearc*=hole or cave, but he does not give the gender of the word. Dineen also has *dearc*=hole, cave, but he makes it feminine with *na dearca* as genitive. Yet note legend 'Cavern' on O.S. maps.

Rahersuck: *An Raithearsach.* I am unable even to suggest a possible explanation of this name.

Reenrourvuar; Reenrourveg: *An Rinn Reamhar Mhór; An Rinn Reamhar Bheag* > *Reamhar* is found in a number of placenames and means 'big', 'rounded', 'solid'. *Rinn*=headland. The meanings are probably 'the big rounded

139

headland' and 'the small rounded headland'.

Rock of the Portuguese: *Carraig an Phoirtingéalaigh.* The English is a direct translation of the Irish name. See Chapter 9 for story of Portuguese captain.

Reenardnagaorach: *Rinn Ard na gCaorach*=The headland of the high ground of the sheep.

Strand of South Harbour: *Tráigh Inbhir Mhóir,* lit.=Strand of the big harbour or haven.

Stocaunnaminaun: *Stocán na Mionnán* : It could mean 'the high isolated rock of the kid goats' but it is far more likely that *mionnán*=a rocky formation like a coronet or crown, and so that the name means 'the high isolated crown-shaped rocks'. Cf. *Mionnán na Gráige* in Corkaguiney (Kerry).

Tayvanvaud: *Taobh an Bháid,* lit.='side of the boat'. Reference may be to the shape of the cliff, or to a particular boat. Former seems more likely.

Tonelinge: *Tón Loinge*='Low lying ground of the ship'. Reference is probably to a ship that was wrecked there.

Toneanamhdaun: *Tón an Amadáin*='The low-lying place of the Fool'. The fool in question may be the one appearing in the folktale of the 'Gruagach' (Wizard) in Chapter 11.

Tonenaginkeenee: *Tón na gCoincíní.* Again *Tón* is=a low-lying place. *Coincín* basically means 'a large upturned nose'. The reference may be to the formation of the coast at the place.

Tracroo: *Tráigh Cru[aidh]* If, as seems likely, the 'Cru' is a contraction of 'Cruaidh' then the meaning of the name would be 'Hard, or Stony Strand' which is an appropriate name for this Sherkin Island strand from which boats set out for *Coosadooglish* in Cape Clear. Alternatively *Crú*= *Cró,* which means 'gore, blood'.

Tradoonclayreh: *Tráigh Dhún Cléire,* lit.='Strand of the Fort of Clear'. The spot is very close to where Ó Síocháin lived, that is the townland of Knockaunnamaurnach, on the north coast of the Island. The fort was probably one of the ancient promontory sort.

Tráigh Ineer: *Tráigh Inbhir*='Strand of the Harbour', that is South Harbour. See *Strand of South Harbour.*

Trakieran: *Tráigh Chiaráin*='St Kieran's Strand', in North Harbour. Pádraig Ó Maidín in his notes on Pococke's Tour comments : 'The fact that the name *Fintracht Cleri* (i.e. Fionn Tráigh Chléire) was superseded by *Tráigh Chiaráin* would appear to indicate that the name *Cléire* was associated with the Island previous to the establishment of devotion to St Ciarán, and was probably pre-Christian' (*J.C.H.A.S.*, 65, 1960, p 140). See *Onomasticon Goedelicum*, s.v. *Finn tracht*, p 422.

Traleagig: *Tráigh Leagaigh*= 'Strand abounding in flat stones', if *Leagaigh* is variation of *Leacach*.

Trageenanlint: *Tráighín an Fhliont'* i.e. 'Little Strand of the Flint Stone'.

Virayduck: *An Bhiréadach*. Apart from noting *bior*=Water, etc. or *bior*=spike, point etc. I can only mention *bairéad*= hat, bonnet, helmet, as possible clues to the name's meaning.

Vunaduck Vuar; Vunaduck Veg: *An Bhunadach Mhór; An Bhunadach Bheag*. I can offer no explanation of *Bunadach*, the key-word in the names.

NOTES

B.Á.C.	Baile Átha Cliath (Dublin).
Béal.	*Béaloideas* (The Journal of the Folklore of Ireland Society), Dublin.
Donovan	*Sketches in Carbery* (County Cork), Daniel Donovan, Dublin, 1876; Cork, 1973.
I.H.S.	*Irish Historical Studies,* Dublin.
I.M.N .	*Irisleabhar Mhuighe Nuadhad, 1929.*
J.C.H.A.S.	*Journal of the Cork Historical and Archaeological Society,* Cork.
Joyce	*A Social History of Ancient Ireland,* P. W. Joyce, Vol. 11, London, 1903.
M.S.H.I.C.	*Manuscript Sources for the History of Irish Civilisation,* Richard J. Hayes, Boston, Mass. (Vol. 6 (1965), p. 37; Vol. 7 (1965), pp 59, 142f., 232).
Miscellany	*Miscellany of the Celtic Society,* ed. John O'Donovan, Dublin, 1849.
O.G.	*Onomasticon Goedelicum,* E. Hogan, S.J., Dublin, 1910.
P.H.	*Pacata Hibernia,* ed. Standish O'Grady, 2 vols., Dublin.
Pococke	'Pococke's Tour of South and South-West Ireland in 1758 (contd.) : Notes', Pádraig Ó Maidín, *J.C.H.A.S.,* 65 (ii), 1960, 130-141.
P.R.I.A.	*Proceedings of the Royal Irish Academy,* Dublin.
S.Ch.	*Seanchas Chléire,* B.Á.C., 1940 (1970, 1973).
Smith	*The Antient and Present State of the County and City of Cork,* in Two Books, Charles Smith, Dublin, 1750 (Republished, Cork, 1973, 2 Vols.).
T.R.I.A.	*Transactions of the Royal Irish Academy,* Dublin.

NOTES TO THE FOREWORD

1. The quotations are from *Labyrinths* (Selected Stories and Other Writings), Penguin Books, 1971, pp 214f., 218.

T. S. Eliot, in his *Notes Towards the Definition of Culture* (London, 1948, pp 53-58), anticipated Borges's thinking, but in the context of the relations of the Celtic peoples of Wales, Scotland, and Ireland to English culture. With his customary finesse—and the rather disingenuous attempt to forestall the objection that he is 'playing a trick'—he threads his way along what some might be persuaded is a pellucid and irrefutable line of argument about the 'satellite cultures' of the three peoples. He advances two reasons for the undesirability of their total assimilation by the stronger culture: 'the instinct of every living thing to persist in its own being,' and 'the satellite exercises a considerable influence upon the stronger culture; and so plays a larger part in the world at large than it could in isolation'.

Although he later states, quite explicitly, that 'there is no safeguard more reliable than a language' for the 'transmission' and 'maintenance' of a culture, he ignores the glaring self-contradiction in a vain effort to reconcile cultural autonomy and linguistic subservience—for the manifest result of the latter cannot be other than 'complete absorption' in the case of the three Celtic peoples.

The whole rationale of his reasoning unfolds itself in one revealing sentence: 'For Ireland, Scotland and Wales to cut themselves off completely from England would be to cut themselves off from Europe and the world ...' It is enough to ask if the Finns and Norwegians have cut themselves off from Europe and the world.

2. The following quotation from C. S. Lewis's *The Discarded Image* (Cambridge, 1970, p 6 f.), is a masterly statement of my point about language:

> Nothing about a literature can be more essential than the language it uses. A language has its own personality; implies an outlook, reveals a mental activity, and has a resonance, not quite the same as those of any other. Not only the vocabulary—*heaven* can never mean quite the same as *ciel*—but the very shape of the syntax is *sui generis*. Hence in the Germanic countries, including England, the debt of the medieval (and modern) literatures to their barbarian origin is all-pervasive. ... In Middle English literature, after every allowance has been made for French and Latin influences, the tone and rhythm and the very 'feel' of every sentence is ... of barbarian descent. Those who ignore the relation of English to Anglo-Saxon as a 'mere philological fact' irrelevant to the literature betray a shocking insensibility to the very mode in which literature exists.

A fortiori, all this is even truer of Irish as there is no call to make allowances for foreign influences which are minimal in comparison with those on English.

I also recommend strongly an essay entitled 'The Relation of Language to Culture' by Harry Hoijer (*Anthropology Today,* Selections, ed. Sol Tax, Univ. of Chicago Press, 1962, pp 258-277).

3. This sentence is from Prof. E. Estyn Evans, *Prehistoric and Early Christian Ireland* (London, 1966, p 34).

All Prof. Evans's writings have an abiding value for they are not limited to a mere presentation of his wide knowledge but move over the threshold of the factual into such value judgements as the following: 'There is ... more continuity with the past in Ireland than in England or most parts of the European mainland' (*ib.,* p 5).

4. I am aware that a potential prototype had already been written in 1915 by An t-Ath. Peadar Ó Laoghaire (Peter O'Leary)—that is *Mo Scéal Féin,* translated in 1970 by Cyril Ó Céirín under the title *My Story* (Mercier Press, Cork). For a number of reasons it had no influence on the later contributors to the autobiographical school, and this was no great harm despite its social, historical, and stylistic merits.

Here is a list of the autobiographies in the chronological order of their first publication—with details about translations into English—where such exists:

> *An t-Oileánach,* Tomás Ó Criomhthain, B.Á.C., 1929,
> (*The Islandman,* Thomas Ó Crohan, Dublin and London, 1937);
> *Fiche Blian ag Fás,* Muiris Ó Suileabháin, B.Á.C., 1933;
> (*Twenty Years A-Growing,* Maurice O'Sullivan, London, 1933);
> *Peig,* Peig Sayers, B.Á.C. agus Corcaigh, 1936,
> (*Peig,* Peig Sayers, Dublin, 1973);
> *Seanchas Chléire,* Conchúr Ó Síocháin, B.Á.C., 1940,
> (*The Man from Cape Clear,* Conchúr Ó Síocháin, Cork, 1975);
> *Scéal mo Bheatha,* Domhnall Bán Ó Céileachair, B.Á.C., 1944,
> (No translation exists);
> *Saol Corrach,* 'Máire' (S. Ó Grianna), B.Á.C., 1945,
> (No translation exists);
> *Rothaí Móra an tSaoil,* Micí Mac Gabhann, B.Á.C., 1959,
> (*The Long Road to Klondyke,* Mícheál Mac Gabhann, London, 1962);
> *Dialann Deoraí,* Dónall Mac Amhlaigh, B.Á.C., 1960,
> (*An Irish Navvy,* Dónall Mac Amhlaigh, London, 1964).

It is well to remind readers that the date of original publication is no clear index to the time of composition. The contents of *Seanchas Chléire* (*The Man from Cape Clear*), for example, were dictated by the author from November 1935 to May 1936.

5. These lines from a poem by Lionel Johnson are quoted from *The Fortunes of the Irish Language,* Daniel Corkery (Cork, 1968, p 127).

They are worth comparing with a stanza by Seán Ó Ríordáin, the most significant of our modern poets in Irish:

Is, mó éag a fuair an teanga so againne,
Ach go brách ní bhfaighidh sí éag ionainne,
Cé minic í ar fionraí
Dár lomdhearg ainneona.
(I add a literal translation of my own:
This tongue of ours has died many a death,
But it will never die in us,
Although it is often in suspension
Despite our most determined will).

Brosna, B.Á.C., 1964 (fifth printing 1970), p 38.

6. *Corcu Loigde* (al. *Corca Laidhe*) is the name of the sept who were 'the foremost representatives of the *Erainn*'. It still survives in the names of two districts bordering on the river Ilen, that is Collymore and Collybeg. These names hold the last tenuous thread that links the O'Driscolls, the chiefs of the *Corcu Loigde,* with their ancient greatness at a time when their rule embraced all south-west Cork or, in modern times, an area roughly co-extensive with the Diocese of Ross.

Owing to encroachments on their territory by other Irish septs (the O'Donovans, the O'Mahonys and the O'Sullivans), which even preceded the effects of the Anglo-Norman invasion, it was whittled down to a stretch of the coast around Baltimore and such islands as Cape Clear and Sherkin. By the early fourteenth century the name *Cairbre* (*angl.* Carbery), the tribal name of the O'Donovans, O'Collins, etc., was beginning to displace that of *Corcu Loigde*.

For further information on the *Corcu Loigde,* Carbery, and Cape Clear, see especially:

Miscellany of the Celtic Society, ed. John O'Donovan, Dublin, 1849.
'The Barony of Carbery', Prof. W. F. T. Butler, *J.C.H.A.S.,* 10, 1904; 1-10, 73-84.
'Early Italian Maps of Ireland; 1300-1600', T. I. Westropp, *P.R.I.A.,* 30, Sec. C, No. 16, 1913.
'The Life and Times of Archbishop Denis O'Driscoll, 1600-1650', Rev. Jas. Coombes, *J.C.H.A.S.,* 70 (1965), 108-119.

The last three items are additional to entries in Section A of the Bibliography.

CHAPTER ONE

1. 'Cp. [The Blaskets] are inhabited by a small population of fishermen of comparatively recent mainland origin' (*The Islandman,* Thomas Ó Crohan, translated from the Irish by Robin Flower, O.U.P., 1951, p vii).

In contrast with this Conchúr Ó Síocháin, *The Man from Cape Clear,* starts and ends his story with the justifiable note of pride in being one of a community whose lineage as continuous occupants of the island roves back over the centuries to Neolithic days (see 'An Example of Passage-grave Art from Co Cork', Michael J. O'Kelly, *J.C.H.A.S.*, 54, 1949, pp 8-10).

Cape Clear has been in the mainstream of the history of Ireland since it was colonised by the *Erainn*, a P-Celtic speaking people, who antedated the Goidels and of whom 'the foremost representatives' were the *Corcu Loigde* of the western part of Co Cork, between the river Bandon and the sea (see *Early Irish History and Mythology*, Thomas F. O'Rahilly, Dublin, 1946).

Indicative, likewise, of this significant difference between Cape Clear and the Blaskets is the fact that Robin Flower is obliged to give in his Foreword to his translation of *An t-Oileánach* some idea of the physical setting of the events in Ó Crohan's narrative, as the Blasketman 'nowhere attempts to describe' the background of his narrative. Ó Síocháin, however, lovingly lingers over every feature of the topography of his island and in plucking the strings of his ancestral memory produces a symphony of legend, chronicle, and lore which is of the island people and not peculiar to himself alone.

I venture to say that Ó Crohan's landscape is almost as bleak and anonymous as that of Golding's *The Inheritors* while Ó Síocháin's reveals not merely all the appeal of a beloved place, but the ageless associations that cling to it.

Ó Crohan's omission of placenames seems to be deliberate, for the author of *Twenty Years Á-Growing* sprinkles his story with a shower of names. In contrast with many of Ó Síocháin's, however, they clearly have such a simple denominative character that it is valid to claim that they are of comparatively recent origin.

2. See:
   (i) 'Hearth and Chimney in the Irish House', C. Ó Danachair, *Béal.*, 16 (i-ii), 1946, 91-104;
   (ii) 'Irish Fields and Houses', Ake Campbell, *Béal.*, 5 (i), 1935, 57-74;
   (iii) 'Some Distributive Patterns in Irish Folk Life', C. Ó Danachair, *Béal.*, 25, 1957, 108-123;
   (iv) 'The Questionnaire System', C. Ó Danachair, *Béal.*, 15 (i-ii), 1945, 203-217.

3. *Train-oil*: A Germanic word which first appears in English in the last years of the fifteenth century. In all the languages in which the word occurs, as well as in the case of the Irish borrowing *troighean,* the meaning is, primarily, 'oil extracted or made to exude'. The *O.E.D.* gives a good illustration for the year 1602: 'They pack the pilchards orderly in hogsheads, which afterwards they press with great weights to the end the traine may soak from them into a vessel placed in the ground to receive it'—Carew, *Cornwall;* and an entry dated 1766 informs us that 'They don't drink train but use it in their lamps.'

Pilchard fishing for the production of train-oil was a very valuable

industry along the south coast from the seventeenth to the nineteenth century, although other fish were also used to produce train-oil. See:
  (i) 'The Irish Pilchard Fishery', Dr A. E. J. Went, *P.R.I.A.*, 51, B5;
  (ii) 'Pilchards in the South of Ireland', Dr A. E. J. Went, *J.C.H.A.S.*, 51, 1946, 137-157;
  (iii) 'The Pilchard Fisheries of South West Cork', Rev. J. Coombes, *J.C.H.A.S.*, 63, 1958, p 117f.
Slige: with reference to the ways in which the train-oil was used to produce light, and the Irish vocabulary involved, see
  (i) the bilingual article: 'Seana-Shoillse na Gaeltachta', S. Ó Duilearga, *Béal.*, 1 (i), 1927, 78-80;
  (ii) 'Bog Wood: A Study in Rural Economy', A. J. Lucas, *Béal.*, 23, 1954, 71-134.

4. Submarine telegraphic communication between Ireland and Britain was successfully established in 1852 or 1853. This helped in providing an interim solution to the problem of speeding up transatlantic communication before 'the realisation of a truly gigantic scheme—the laying of a cable from the Old World to the New' (*Telegraphy and Telephony,* A. Williams, London, 1928, p 66). I have failed in my efforts to discover the date when the submarine link with Cape Clear was made and the practice of having all east-bound transatlantic vessels call at the island introduced. This lasted until at least 28 July 1866 when Valentia in Co Kerry was permanently linked by cable with Heart's Content in Newfoundland, and a dream thus realised after seven years of frustrated efforts.
A consequence of the island's key position in these years preceding 1866 was that people learned all about 'the battles, sieges, victories, and defeats' in the course of the American Civil War, and heard about the assassination of Lincoln in 1865 before anyone else in Europe. See also:
  (i) *From Semaphore to Satellite,* Published by the International Telecommunication Union, Geneva, n.d. (37-39);
  (ii) *Submarine Telegraphy,* D. H. Cameron, London, 1927.

5. O'Donovan Rossa (1831-1915)—an indomitable Irishman. See:
  (i) *Rossa's Recollections 1838-1898,* Introduced by Seán Ó Luing, Shannon, 1972;
  (ii) *Diarmuid Ó Donnabháin Rosa:* A Character Study, Dublin, 1915.

6. Similar quatrains were composed by Fr Labhrás Ó Mathúna (Laurence O'Mahony) when he was passing through the sound in the early nineteenth century on his journey to Cape Clear to take up a curacy there—reluctantly it would appear (see *Irisleabhar na Gaeilge,* Márta 1908, p 129). Fr Ó Mathúna is remembered by the islanders as a poet, and Ó Síocháin tells us a little about the man and his verse in Chapter Nine.
See 'Cape Clear Couplet-custom', *J.C.H.A.S.*, 1, 1892, p 185.

7. The best accounts of Morty Oge's life are:
   (i) *Seanchas na Deasmhumhan* (Cab. 22), Domhnall Ó Súilleabháin, B.Á.C., 1940;
   (ii) 'Morty Oge O'Sullivan—Captain of the Wild Geese', John O'Mahony, *J.C.H.A.S.*, 1, 1892, 95-99, 116-127, 249.

Morty Oge (1710ca.-1754) led a life of the most intriguing sort, one having all the contrast of shade and light in a chiaroscudo painting. It is a mystery that such a fascinating figure has failed to attract the atten.ion of a true historical novelist.

He was born at Coulagh (*Cuailleach*) near the village of Eyeries (*Na hAedharaí*) in West Cork, and probably received his education on the Continent. Between spells spent at home he fought on the side of Queen Maria Theresa in the War of Austrian Succession in 1738-39 during which the Empress herself presented him with a costly mounted sword as a token of her appreciation of the courage he displayed on her behalf. Later he fought under Lord Clare at Fontenoy (1745) where he was appointed Colonel on the battlefield for his bravery, at Culloden (1746), and at Lauffield (1747).

The contrast between the man who 'wore a suit of gold lace by being the finest man in France' and Morty, the West Cork scion of a noble family, now reduced when in his native land to being a pirate, smuggler, and recruiting officer for the Irish Brigade is dramatic; and equally so is the ultimate sequel to that persistent homing call that turned him into a man 'on his keeping'. This dramatic diptych is intensified by the contrast between the woman who keened over his dead body, and the mother of a dead young recruit to the Wild Geese who reviled and cursed the corpse for his being responsible for enlisting her son.

The tragic end to Morty's fascinating life came on 4 May 1754 as a result of his having killed the revenue officer John Puxley who, ironically, lived in the great O'Sullivan Beare's fortress of Dunboy Castle. On that day—betrayed by the inevitable traitor—he was surrounded in his house by forty soldiers who had come from Cork in a naval vessel called the *Speedwell*. Ultimately the house was fired, and when Morty rushed out, after companions had done likewise earlier to confuse the attackers, he was shot by one Sam Swete. Morty's deep appeal as a patriotic figure in his own right, and as an offspring of a noble Irish clan, as well as the sorrow at the indignity meted out to his dead body, are well conveyed by Ó Síocháin. After his corpse was brought to Cork he was decapitated and while his head was spiked on the South Gate Bridge Prison wall as a 'show' for the gentry and a warning to the natives, his body was buried in Cat Fort.

There is a story that Morty's only son, Seán na hInse, was rewarded by the authorities for defending a lady against a crowd of ruffians by being granted any favour he requested. The one he sought was his father's spiked head for decent burial.

8. If we include this version of the lament composed by Donal O'Con-

nell, Morty's foster-brother, and another containing thirteen stanzas (published by Donal Ua hÉilí in the periodical *Loch Léin,* Cill Áirne, Bealtaine 1904), there are—as far as I can make out—six versions or part-versions extant. The remainder are : one in the *J.C.H.A.S.* article mentioned in the last note (12 verses); one in *Cois na Ruachtaí* (Risteárd Ó Foghlú, B.Á.C., 1938—12 verses); one in the *Seanchas na Deasmhumhan* chapter, also referred to in the last note; and, finally, a very defective fragmentary version in *The Last Colonel of the Irish Brigade,* Mrs M. J. O'Connell, London, 1892 (Vol. 2, p 345f.).

There are four other elegies on Morty Oge, three in Irish and one in English. Two of those in Irish may be found in *Diarmuid na Bolgaí agus a Chomhursain* (Seán Ó Súilleabháin, B.Á.C., 1937), one composed by Diarmuid na Bolgaí Ó Sé himself (No. 30, 84-87), the other a defective one from oral tradition (*ib.,* 197-198). The third was the work of Sean-Mhícheál Ó Longáin and may be found in *Cois na Ruachtaí,* pp 79-83.

Perhaps the best-known of all the laments is the 'Dirge of O'Sullivan Bear' by Jeremiah J. Callanan (see *A Treasury of Irish Poetry in the English Language,* ed. Stopford A. Brooke and T. W. Rolleston, 1905, 93-94). Although this is stated to be from the Irish I know nothing about the existence of such an origin for this poem which is certainly impressive for the fire and passion of its rhetoric.

CHAPTER TWO

1. *Taft* not *thwart* (Ir. *tochta*) is the word in common use in the neighbouring island of Sherkin. The English words have different origins. The *O.E.D.* records *taft* only for the Shetlands and the Isle of Man, and says that it is one of a number of Northern English dialect words which are now obsolete in R.S.E., in which it was absorbed by *thwart* in the thirties of the eighteenth century.

2. *An Seabhac* (P. Ó Siochrú) describes both games in 'Cluichí Leanbh sa Ghaeltacht', *Béal.,* 12, 1942, 29-54 ('Buttons', p 35 f., quoits, p 32). See also (i) 'Children's Games', Pádraig Ó Conchubhair, in *Béal.,* 17 (i-ii), 1947, 186-200 (p 194f.), and (ii) *Irish Heritage,* E. Estyn Evans, Dundalk, 1947, p 52 *et passim.* Evans refers on p 175 to the use of a 'bull-roarer' (*cláirín búirthe*)—formerly an ancient ceremonial instrument—as a toy on Cape Clear. As far as I am aware it is not known in the Kerry Gaeltacht; nor is the article mentioned in Dineen's *Foclóir.*

3. 'Big Bartholomew's day' (*Lá Pharthaláin Mhóir*) is explained as any day in which something is to be done about which we feel anxious, e.g. the examination day in a school (see p 70 in 'Dornán Cnuais Ó Chuantaibh Chléire' by Rev. D. Ó Floinn in *I.M.N.,* 1929, 62-73). Who was Parthalán, and why should his name connote anxiety or worry? The answer, I think, is to be attributed to the likelihood that we have here an example of the incredible tenacity of the folk memory in a community whose ancestry stretches back to pre-historic times. The name Parthalán parallels, imaginatively, at any rate, the Cape Clear decorated stone mentioned in Note 1 of the first chapter. In the *Lebor Gabala (Book of Conquests)*, which is a learned construct, the role of the earliest invader of Ireland after the Flood is filled by Parthalán. The element of anxiety linked with his name is possibly a consequence of the detail of his legend that he and his people were wiped out by a plague and left no descendants. (See *Early Irish History and Mythology,* Thomas F. O'Rahilly, Dublin, 1946, p 75 *et passim,* for an authoritative analysis of this and other 'learned inventions' as well as of the true history of ancient Ireland.)

CHAPTER THREE

1. Describing Cape Clear in 1750 Charles Smith wrote: 'The north side bears potatoes, barley and a little wheat, and the south is mostly a craggy rock ... They have a good quantity of sheep and cows, some swine and horses, but all their cattle are very small' (pp 286, 287).
See the following contributions to *Béal.*:
  (i) 'The Spade in Ireland', C. Ó Danachair, 31, 1963, 98-114;
  (ii) 'Foclóir agus Téarmaí Feirmeoireachta', S. Ó Dubhda, 13, 1943, 3-39;
  (iii) 'Téarmaí agus Seanchas Feirmeoireachta', C. Ó Muimhneacháin, 14, 1944, 3-44;
  (iv) Works of E. Estyn Evans listed in the Bibliography.

2. *Doolamaun* and *Loke* (Ir. *Dúlamán* and *Lóch*): two of the numerous species of algae found on the shores and rocks of Cape Clear.
Doolamaun is Bladder Wrack (*Fucus vesiculosus*), and *loke* is seathongs (*Himanthalia elongata*). See:
  (i) *The Natural History of Cape Clear Island,* ed. J. T. R. Sharrock, Berkhamstead, 1973, 183-185;
  (ii) *Phycology of the South Coast of Ireland,* J. P. Cullinane, Cork, 1973.

3. 'Our lord in this world': Until the Land Acts (from 1881 onwards) reduced gradually the hold of the landlord classes on their vast estates the Bechers were the overlords of Cape Clear, Sherkin and of immense areas of County Cork. There is a traditional saying that one could once walk on Becher land all the way from Castlehaven to Cork City. The first member of this particular branch of the breed of predatory planters to acquire property in Ireland was one Fane (Phane) Becher who, after the suppression of the Munster rebellion in 1583, received a grant of 14,000 acres in County Cork by a warrant dated 3 February 1586-87. His eldest son, Henry, of Castle Mahon, Co. Cork, was Lord President of Munster in 1604. This man's eldest son bore the same name and came into possession of the estate of Aughadown on the banks of the River Ilen by marriage. The last of the early Bechers who merits some mention was this second Henry's son, Colonel Thomas, who was A.D.C. to William III at the Battle of the Boyne where the king presented him with his gold and silver watch as a mark of appreciation of his dutiful service. Needless to say this gift has been a treasured possession of the descendants of Thomas who himself settled down in Sherkin Island as Governor of the Barrack there. The site of this establishment was within the walls of the old O'Driscoll castle of Dun na Long (now called the Garrison) which according to Dive Downes, the Protestant bishop of Cork and Ross who paid a visit to the island in August 1699, was still a strong place of defence 'having 2 or 3 platforms towards the sea, whereon are about 8 guns planted' ('Bishop Dive Downes' Visitation of his Diocese, 1699', ed. T. A. Lunham, *J.C.H.A.S.*, 14, 1908, p 143).

The family vault of the Bechers may be seen in the Aughadown grave-yard of the old Church of St Matthew built in 1814 and abandoned for a better-placed building dedicated to the same saint in 1873. See:

(i) *The Pooles of Mayfield,* Rosemary ffolliott, Dublin, 1958, 240f.;

(ii) *Burkes Landed Gentry of Ireland,* ed. L. G. Pine, London, 4th ed., 1958, 72-73;

(iii) *English Money and Irish Land,* Karl S. Bottigheimer, Oxford, 1973.

4. 'The Song of Treason', unlike the far better known 'Lament for Morty Oge', does not appear to have survived in any other written version.

5. *Old Court* : The remains of an O'Driscoll castle are still to be seen here from the road between Skibbereen and Baltimore. After the disaster of Kinsale the place appears to have been seized and occupied by Captain Stafford, one of Sir George Carew's men (see *P.H.*, Vol. 2, p 213). On the submission of Sir Fineen O'Driscoll after his brief toying with 'disloyaltie' (*ib.*, p 41) his eldest son Connor remained loyal to the Irish cause and fled to Spain with the famous Jesuit James Archer. See:

(i) *Distinguished Irishmen of the Sixteenth Century,* Edmond Hogan, S.J.;

(ii) 'The Old Castles of South-West Cork', James Coleman, *J.C.H.A.S.*, 31, 1926, 45-47;

(iii) 'The Life and Times of Bishop Denis O'Driscoll, 1600-1650', Rev. J. Coombes, *J.C.H.A.S.*, 70, 1965, 108-119.

Sir Fineen's being offered 'all kind and mild usage' by Queen Elizabeth did not save his ancient and noble family from losing all their possessions in Carbery and falling into decay. Shortly after 1603 Sir Fineen 'let Baltimore and the whole of Collymore [Ir.: *Cothluidhe Mór*] territory to a certain Thomas Crooke for 21 years' (see *Miscellany,* p 390).

6. The tradition of execution for the most trivial offence is still remembered in Sherkin Island, but is associated with a spot in Aughadown called *Árd na gCrochairí* (Hangman's Height), and not with Old Court.

7. *Abbeystrewery* (Ir. *Mainistir Bhéal na Sruthra*): This was one of the fifty-four early Cistercian foundations in Ireland.

I cannot forbear quoting the following: 'The new surging vitality of the Cistercians carried their order into every sector of Irish life. In 1157, fifteen years after its foundation, Church and State combined to make the consecration of the abbey church in Mellifont one of the most resplendent occasions of the age, graced by the presence of the King of Ireland and the Archbishop of Armagh, seventeen bishops and several princes of the land. The king presented the monastery with seven score cows, three score ounces of gold and a townland near Drogheda' (*A History of Timoleague and Barryroe,* Rev. James Coombes, Timoleague, 1969, p 13f.).

The story of the foundation of the Cistercian monastery of De Fonte Vivo at Abbeymahon in the diocese of Ross in 1172, down to its suppression in 1537, is told briefly by Fr Coombes in the same booklet (p 14). Abbeystrewery (De Flumine Vivo), another Cistercian foundation, was the only daughter-house of Abbeymahon, and all the information we have about it is that a decree of the Cistercian Chapter-General in 1281 ordered that the 'place called De Flumine Vivo, shall be restored as an Abbey of the order and be, as it formerly was, the daughter of Fons Vivus'. I am indebted to my friend Fr Coombes for his permission to make free use of the information in his booklet.

By 1876 nothing remained of Abbeystrewery but 'gray crumbling walls, covered with moss and lichens' (Donovan, p 29). See:
  (i) 'Obligationes pro Annatis Diocesis Rossensis', ed. James Coombes, *Archivium Hibernicum,* 29, 1970, 33-48 (p 42, f.n. 26);
  (ii) *Pococke* (132-133).

8. For the history of travel in Ireland see:
  (i) *Charles Bianconi, 1786-1875 (A Biography),* Mrs Morgan J. O'Connell, London, 1878;
  (ii) *Bianconi, King of the Irish Roads,* M. O'C. Bianconi and S. J. Watson, Dublin, 1962;
  (iii) *A Seat behind the Coachman (Travellers from 1800 to 1900),* Diarmuid Ó Muirithe, Dublin, 1972;
  (iv) *Travel and Transport in Ireland,* ed. Kevin B. Nowlan, Dublin and New York, 1973.

CHAPTER FOUR

1. Chapters 4-6, inclusively, preserve much valuable information about fishing and the lives of fishermen during the late nineteenth and early twentieth centuries, thus adding to the source material available not only for the social historian but for the Irish lexicographers, because Dineen's seminal, even magisterial Dictionary is wanting in words peculiar to the people of Cape Clear. The compiler of any future dictionary of Irish will find supplementary material from Cape Clear in Rev. D. Ó Floinn's bilingual essay 'Dornán Cnuais ó Chuantaibh Chiéire', *I.M.N.* (1929, 62-73), especially with regard to fish and fishing, s.v.v. *bád* and *iasc*.

See also: 'Seanchas Iascaireachta agus Farraige', Seán Ó hEochaidh, *Béal.*, 33, 1965, 1-96. There is an editorial summary in English on pp 87-92.

2. There is a fine collection of adages (103 in all), and of proverbs (165 in all) from Cape Clear in 'Béaloideas ó Chléire II', D. Ó Floinn, *Béal.*, 11 (i-ii), 1941, 58-75.

3. A description of the ways in which various species of fish were counted may be found in the article mentioned in the previous note, 37-38.

CHAPTER FIVE

1. According to a reliable informant in Sherkin Island, Michael MacCarthy, this make of fishing boat was a dandy-rigged ketch or yawl such as was a common sight in European waters from 1700-1900. The same person was able to name some of the Cape Clear fleet which, owing to the generosity of the philanthropist Baroness Burdett-Coutts, the Cape Clear fishermen were able to acquire from the late 1870s onwards: *Roving Swan, Guiding Star, Blue Jacket, Saggart Aroon, Saor Ghael, St Ciaran, St Patrick, San Columba, Pride of Erin.* He also told me that these craft were built in the boat-building yards of Watson and Graves in the Isle of Man.

2. *Baffity*: William Norris, another Sherkin Island man, to who I am indebted for information about this and much else besides, remembers the word. Baffity was a cheap cotton or calico fabric which was steeped in linseed oil and treated with egg yolks in order to provide the only protective clothing fishermen had until modern oilskins were introduced.

The word is of Persian origin and probably came into Irish from *boffeta*, a sixteenth century form of the English loan word. See *O.E.D.*, sv. *Baft*.

3. See 'The Craft of Coopering', J. C. Coleman, *J.C.H.A.S.*, 49, 1944, 79-89.

4. In the medieval period Ireland's most valuable export trade to England and the Continent consisted of fish, principally pilchards, hake, cod, herring and salmon. Indeed until the disaster of Kinsale (1601) a valuable source of income for the O'Driscolls, the hereditary chieftains of Carbery, was the rent paid by foreign fishermen who came to the coast. While pilchard fishing was particularly rewarding in the seventeenth and early eighteenth centuries, it is clear from the evidence of Smith (1750) and Pococke (1758) that by their time the trade in pilchards had declined and that the fish 'palaces' in Cape Clear were no longer needed for 'of late years there has not a single Pilchard appeared on the coast' (Smith, 292f.). Cod, hake, ling and mackerel then took the place of pilchards in importance, and of these hake continued to be increasingly caught until immense shoals of mackerel began to swarm around the coast in the late nineteenth and early twentieth centuries. During this period, and especially in the years of the First World War, mackerel fishing prospered and enormous quantities were exported, especially to Canada and the United States. Catches of 60,000 were common at the height of the boom. With the return of the English trawlers in the post-war period and the collapse of the American market in the 1920s the fishermen of Cape Clear faced a disaster which is reflected in the decline in population that continued until recent years, when the recovery of fishing under the aegis of Bord Iascaigh Mhara—and other encouraging factors in the island's life— have at least halted the disastrous drop in population. See:

 (i) 'Pilchards in the South-West of Ireland', A. E. J. Went, *J.C.H.A.S.*, 69, 1964;
 (ii) 'The Pilchard Fisheries of South West Cork', Rev. J. Coombes, *J.C.H.A.S.*, 63, 1958, 117f.;
(iii) 'The Irish Hake Fishery 1504-1824', A. E. J. Went, *J.C.H.A.S.*, 51, 1946, 41-51;
(iv) 'The Irish Pilchard Fishery', A. E. J. Went, *P.R.I.A.*, 51, B5;
 (v) 'Pilchards in the South of Ireland', A. E. J. Went, *J.C.H.A.S.*, 51, 1946, 137-157;
(vi) *A Handbook of Irish Folklore*, Seán Ó Súilleabháin, Dublin, 1942 (A bilingual list of Irish fish-names may be found on pp 297-300);
(vii) 'Dornán Cnuais ó Chuantaibh Cléire', D. Ó Floinn, *I.M.N.*, 62-76 (Cf. fish-names s.v. *iasc* on p 68 with the list in vi).

CHAPTER SIX

1. The date of this storm is given as 1892 in all three editions of the original Irish—a lapse of memory on the narrator's part which I was enabled to correct through the help of my two friends from Sherkin Island, William Norris and Michael MacCarthy. Both were adamant that the year of the gale was 1894. And so it proved to be, as I established from a report in the *Cork Examiner* of Thursday, 26 April 1894, in which the details correspond closely and conclusively with those in Ó Síocháin's narrative.

2. 'Shegwee' < Ir. *sí-gaoith* = a whirlwind, a sudden blast of wind, a fairy wind.

3. 'Truly terrifying sights': If translation were merely a matter of finding direct verbal equivalences then I should have used the personal name 'Murrough' (*Murchadh* in Irish) here; but that would have conveyed nothing to the reader unfamiliar with Irish history. Indeed if I had written 'a Gorgan' it would have been more comprehensible. Murrough O'Brien (1614-74), the sixth Baron and first Earl of Inchiquin, was a direct lineal descendant of Brian Boru, Ireland's warrior king. Murrough was educated and brought up as a Protestant in England and on his return this renegade vented his implacable hatred of Catholicism on the people in such a spate of merciless incendiarism and atrocities that he became known as *Murchadh na dTóiteán* (Murrough of the Burnings). His reputation in folk memory as an inhuman monster has been aptly put by John A. Murphy (see 'The Sack of Cashel 1647', *J.C.H.A.S.*, 70, 55-62): 'If Cromwell was execrated by the folk memory of the nation at large, Inchiquin was similarly anathemised in Munster tradition' (*ib.*, 55). Consequently one may use the word 'Murchadh' in Irish as a synonmy for severe pain, real terror, or truly daunting trouble.

In addition to Prof. Murphy's article see:

(i) *The Irish Catholic Confederacy and the Puritan Revolution,* Thomas T. Coonan, Columbia U.P., 1954;

(ii) *Ireland under the Stuarts, 1603-1690,* Richard Bagwell, 3 vols., London, 1906-1916.

(iii) *Cromwell in Ireland: A History of Cromwell's Irish Campaign,* Denis Murphy, Dublin, 1883 (excellent).

The Blasket Island imprecation *Marbhadh an Dúna ort!* carries with it its own untranslatable legacy of historical undertones.

CHAPTER SEVEN

1. My Sherkin Island friends still remember the stories of this smuggler, and call him 'Lord John'. He is not named in my original.

(i) 'The Smuggling Trade in Ireland in the Eighteenth Century', F. G. James, *I.H.S.*, 12, 299-317.

An item listed in *M.S.H.I.C.* (ed. R. J. Hayes, Vol. 7, Places A-K, 1965, p 232) is of particular interest: 'Proposal for better securing the West Indian trade and for hindering commerce between France and Ireland, and giving the Irish a considerable disturbance in the South near Cape Clear', n.d. Essay for a test against whigs: addressed to the Duke of Ormonde n.d. (Dublin: Trinity College Lib. MS 1180 (i 610): (Extracts)).

2. Some justification for the translation is called for as the idiom might well appear to be of purely English origin. Eric Partridge

(*A Dictionary of Slang,* Vol. I, London, 1963) has no more to say about the phrase than that it means 'to finish in a manner regarded as objectionable to the speaker', and that it dates from 1916; this clearly suggests a military provenance, and he equates it with 'to put the tin hat (=helmet) on ...' No further attempt is made by him to explain its origin or evolution in meaning.

When we turn to the original Irish of our text we find that the *barracinn dúda* is simply 'the pipe-cover', formerly the common tin cap of a *dúd* (dim. *dúidín*). Again the semantic development which produced precisely the same sense as the English phrase is something I am unable to explain. It does, however, clearly appear that this Irish idiom predates 1916; and so we are left with a problem which experts in Hiberno-English may be able to solve. Dineen—it should be added—does not record the idiom so that its apparent restriction to the Cape Clear dialect adds a further complication which may well mean that it was introduced into the Irish of the Island subsequent to the war and transposed into their own homely idiom.

3. 'Angishore' (<Ir. *ainniseoir*) is quite common in Hiberno-English, and may be translated 'poor fellow', 'wretch', etc.; but no English word can quite convey the expressive and emotive undertones of the Irish word.

CHAPTER EIGHT

1. This proverb is widely diffused in European literature. I have come across it in Chaucer and Provencal poetry, and it is so long in existence that it occurs in the works of Aeschylus and Aesop.

2. 'White horse' (Ir. *Capall bán*), meaning summons or document, is a euphemistic phrase which reminds me of the Blasket phrase for worms i.e. *buachaillí geala* (=white boys). The overtones are quite different.

3. The original Irish, *scrál,* is probably derived from the English 'scrawl', a word which would be familiar to schoolchildren in the last century because of the special emphasis placed on achieving the ideal of a copperplate style in writing. 'Scrawl' might then readily be used of an untidy heap of the long lines of fishermen. This hypothesis was developed from a hint conveyed to me by Prof. Pádraig Ó Fiannachta of Maynooth College.

CHAPTER NINE

1. *Carriglure* (Ir. *Carrig Liuir*): The explanation of this place-name given by the narrator in Chapter Ten—namely that a *liuir* was a kind

156

of French fishing boat that frequented the coast 'a long time ago' may well be accurate. We should then, perhaps, derive the Irish word from French *lougre* (<Engl. *lugger*). The argument for this derivation is strengthened by Ó Síocháin's reference to the craft's having three lug sails on each of its three masts.

2. A reference to one of the four 'gallawns', or menhirs, in Comillane, the further east of the island's sixteen townlands. This is the only one of these pillar-stones that has an aperture. and it is called *Cloch na Geallúna* (The Trysting Stone) where, in the words of Donovan, 'couples plighted their troth by shaking hands through the aperture'. He also adds that the 'gallawn' was 'a venerable relic connected in some way or other with the worship of the Druids' (Donovan, p 113). P. Ó Maidín appositely quotes a passage from Prof. Seán Ó Ríordáin's *Antiquities of the Irish Countryside* (3rd ed., London, 1953, p 81): 'Certain highly ornamented stones of Early Iron Age date ... were undoubtedly cult objects. So also are holed standing stones with some of which superstitious practices are said to have been associated' (quoted in *Pococke,* p 159f.).
A description of these particular stones and other 'gallawns' and antiquities on the island may be found in 'Cape Clear Island', J. P. Conlon, *J.C.H.A.S.*, 24, 56-60.

3. *Lockaleen* (Ir. *Loch an Lín*=The Flax Pond). Smith comments: 'But what is most pleasing, the linen manufacture has got some footing in this island, for I have seen tolerable crops of flax; most of the women spin, and it is said that they purge and whiten their yarn to a degree of perfection by means of the soft water of the lake before mentioned' (i.e. Loch Iriol, for which see Chapter Eleven, Note 1), (Vol. 1, 289). See also:
(i) *Donovan,* 110f.;
(ii) *Irish Folk Ways,* E. Estyn Evans, London and Boston, 1972, 159ff.;
(iii) *Joyce,* Vol. 11, 354-6.

4. *Conchúr Mac Eireamháin:* There can be little doubt about the actual existence of this eight foot giant of the O'Driscoll line whatever fabulous accretions his feats have acquired in the folk memory. His grave is still pointed out in the cemetery of Killkieran. See:
(i) *Donovan,* p 114f.;
(ii) 'Béaloideas ó Chléire II', D. Ó Floinn, *Béal.,* (i-ii), 1941, 34-37.

5. Fr Laurence O'Mahony (Ir. *Labhrás Ó Mathúna*): one of the succession of priests who in Penal and post-Penal times ministered in both Cape Clear and Sherkin Island, which were treated as a separate mission until 1831. The combined population of the islands in that year was in excess of two thousand.
Just as Cape Clear had its 'king' (always an O'Driscoll) and its own

code of laws down to 1730, it must have had its official *file* (poet), and I remember an islandman whose soubriquet was *An file*.

The name of another poet, Séamus na Struma Ó Réagáin survives in the island's lore, and it is no surprise to discover that the poet Cearúl Ó Dálaig, about whom legends abound in Munster, is reputed to have spent a spell on the island as a weaver.

6. A much longer version of 'Love of my Heart' (*Laogh mo Chroí*) was published by Torna (one-time Prof. of Irish at University College, Cork) in *Irisleabhar na Gaeilge* (1908, 109-110) and contains ten stanzas. The last stanza here is not however included in Torna's text.

7. *Ríobún* is made out of pure hulled wheat grain which is roasted in a bastible, then ground in a quern and mixed with fresh milk, and seasoned. The process is described in Chapter Ten.

The islanders used other methods of treating the wheat grain to produce two other popular 'dishes', *gráinseachán* and *próinsimín* (also *probhainsimí*). The former was made by boiling unground grain in water; milk or sugar was then sometimes added. The latter was hardened or toasted grain which was then eaten with sugar without adding milk. This last appears to have been especially attractive to children as they missed no chance of snatching a few fistfulls in order to make it. Cf. *Proinnseachán* (etc.) and *gráinseachán* in Dineen, and the English *frumenty* or *furmety*.

Querns (pronounced 'quarns' in Sherkin Island, just as 'quoits' is pronounced 'quates'): The original Irish *bró* is a cognate word. Handmills, known in Ireland from Neolithic times, when they took the primitive form of crude grain-rubbers, were used everywhere throughout the land—as references in the Brehon Laws show. They continued in use until comparatively recent times, indeed into the present century. For the terminology in Modern Irish see 'Foclóir agus Téarmaí Feirmeoireachta', Seán Ó Dubhda, *Béal.*, 13 (i-ii), 1943, 3-39 (p 28).

CHAPTER TEN

1. Quarantine Hill (*Cnoc Coraintín*): I have certain reservations about the correctness of Rev. J. Coombes logical and well-documented elucidation of the origin of this place-name (*Dinnseanchas*, 1 (No. 2), 1964, 55-56). He claims that since 'Baltimore was the quarantine port for Cork for at least 73 years that it is hardly necessary to look further for the origin of the names in question', i.e. Quarantine Island (N.E. of Sherkin), and Quarantine Hill. He concludes that 'the hill was probably used as a look-out post.'

Dineen's *Dictionary* includes no reference in his entry for the word for, while the fascicules of the *R.I.A. Contributions* containing 'co-' has not yet been published, Dr E. C. Quinn has been good enough to

158

inform me that no examples of the word have been recorded for it. See:

(i) 'The Leper-Hospitals of Munster', Gerard A. Lee, *North Munster Antiquarian Journal*, 10, 12-25;

(ii) 'Comments on the History of Leprosy', J. Lowe, *Indian Medical Gazette*, 33 (1942);

(iii) 'Medieval Leprosy in the British Isles', W. P. MacArthur, *Journal of the Royal Army Medical Corps of Britain*, 45 (1925).

2. *French furze* : what distinguishes it from irish furze is that it is coarser and bushier. A special machine was used for crushing and mincing the shoots of the furze so that it could be fed to horses and cows.

See: 'Furze: A Survey and History of its Uses in Ireland', A. T. Lucas, *Béal.*, 26 (1958).

3. *Kedge Island* : The original Irish is *Oileán Dhúnlaing* (=Dowling's, Dooley's, Doolin's Island). In *The Statistical Survey of the County of Cork* (H. Townsend, Dublin, 1810) the map facing the title page calls the island 'Dooly Rock'. In the *Miscellany*, published thirty-nine years later, there is a map of *Corca Laidhe* (the O'Driscoll territory in West Cork) in which Kedge Rock is named 'Doolig' or 'Cairgin in Dolaigh', a title which, despite its corrupt form, is clearly related to Ó Síocháin's *Oileán Dhúnlaing*. See *Kedge Island* and *Toe Head* in the 'Appendix on Placenames'.

In the *Miscellany* also 'Dunlaing' appears as the name of one of the hereditary leaders of a region of indeterminate extent stretching eastwards and westwards from Glandore Head (*Ceann Mara*). The name also occurs a number of times in the genealogies of the Corca Laidhe, both lay and episcopal (*ib.*, 10, *et passim*). The name 'Kedge Island' is clearly of comparatively recent origin. See also: *Miscellany*, 87-92.

4. I have found it impossible to reconcile the figures given in some sources for the island's population with the official nineteenth and twentieth centuries decennial census returns that I have examined.

Smith, the earliest source I have consulted, stated that there were 400 families in Cape Clear, a figure which should produce any total between 1,200 and 2,000 (1750 , Vol. 1, 287), the lower figure of which is given as the minimum population, sixty years later, as computed by H. Townsend (*Statistical Survey of the County of Cork,* Dublin, 1810). According to the official census figures Townsend's total had declined by 1841 to 1,052; thenceforth to 1911 the figures were as follows:— 1851, pop. 819; 1861, pop. 736; 1871, pop. 572; 1881, pop. 592; 1891, pop. 584; 1901, pop. 571; 1911, pop. 565. These figures speak for themselves, and when we recall that the present population is no more than 180 it would almost seem vain to expect that Cape Clear can eventually escape the fate of the Blasket Islands. Yet there is every reason for hope as in Cape Clear the leadership of a spirited priest has given the islanders an inspiring vision of their heritage, dignity, and rights. At the same time the island, like the whole country, is benefiting from improved economic and social conditions and vastly improved fishing, so that a real upsurge in population is possible.

See *Seanchas ón Oileán Tiar,* T. Ó Criomhthain (eag. S. Ó Duilearga), B.Á.C., 1956, p 262f.

5. The most recent publication on Irish lighthouses—*The Irish Lighthouse Service,* T. G. Wilson, Dublin, 1968—states that 'in 1810 there was a lighthouse on the highest point of Cape Clear' (p 35). This is not quite accurate as the remains show that it was built on Knockeenatowick (*Cnoicín an tSeabhaic*) near the highest cliff and not on Quarantine Hill (*Cnoc Coraintín*). It was the very first lighthouse on the south coast.

The high elevation meant, however, that the light was always badly obscured in thick or foggy weather so that it was of no use at all on far too many occasions, although its powerful revolving light of 21 lamps was visible at a distance of 28 nautical miles in clear weather. By 1847 when it became a matter of urgency to build a new lighthouse, the site chosen was the Fastnet Rock (*Carraig Aonair*)—three to four miles south-west of Cape Clear.

The work began in 1848 and was completed in 1854. The cast-iron tower on the Rock proved unequal to the fury of the elements, and so it had to be strengthened—a task which lasted from 1865 to 1868. Even this careful and thorough-going improvement could not conceal the basic deficiencies of the structure, and so the whole tower was replaced by a superbly built granite edifice, the construction of which went on from 1899 to 1903. At last 'one of the most beautiful lighthouses in the world' began for the first time to turn its spokes of welcome light for the benefit of all mariners in July 1904. See:

(i) *A Brief Description of Cape Clear,* R. Wilson, Jr., Cork, 1832;

(ii) *Donovan,* 107f.

6. Donovan (p 109) and James M. Burke ('Cape Clear Island', *J.C.H.A.S.,* 14 (2nd series), 1908, 121) agree that the Signal Tower 'of fortress-like appearance' was erected very shortly after the storm-battered remnants of the French fleet that had set out from Brest arrived, with Hoche and Tone, in Bantry in December 1796. Similar towers were built elsewhere on the coast, the nearest being Spain Tower south of Baltimore.

The existence of a manuscript 'map of the ground occupied by a signal tower and the road leading to it at Cape Clear ... surveyed by John Hampton', and dated October 1806 (*M.S.H.I.C.,* ed. R. Hayes, Vol. 7. Places A-K, Boston, 1965, 232, E.), shows that the tower built close to the lighthouse was constructed during the previous decade.

7. The False Men (*Na Fir Bréagacha*): Concerning this *ruse de querre*
—see
  (i) 'Cape Clear Island', Jas. M. Burke, *J.C.H.A.S.*, 14 (2nd series),
      1908, 121;
 (ii) 'Cape Clear Island', J. P. Conlon, *J.C.H.A.S.*, 24 (2nd series),
      1918, 53;
(iii) *Donovan*, 109f.

8. Fastnet Rock (=*Carraig Aonach* in the original Irish): In the
seventeenth century the English name for the rock was either 'Fasteney',
'Fashney' or 'Fastness' (*Miscellany*, 99, 103, 104). While these forms
may be explained with relative ease one used in the fourteenth century,
i.e. 'Fres', defies explanation. From 1500 on, however, the Portolan
Maps have some form like 'Fastenay'. The Irish also presents problems
as the second element in the name is not readily comprehensible as it
stands. It may well be that the guttural at the end is intrusive and a
late accretion and that we thus should really have here the name
Eanna which is found in the Corca Laidhe genealogies (*Miscellany*,
18 *et passim*). There is an alternative Irish form *Carraig Aonair*
(=The Lone or Single Rock), which makes acceptable sense.

9. 'The jealous hands': in essentials this version of the death of Diarmuid retains the story line of the conclusion of the literary *Tóraíocht*
or *Pursuit of Diarmuid and Gráinne,* the masterly and best-loved story
of the Fenian Cycle, although it reveals the folk tendency to introduce
local colouring.
The Fenian tales, either as ballads or prose, with far deeper roots in
popular tradition than the Mythological or Red Branch tales, developed later than these latter and retained their hold on the Irish imagination down to our own times.

10. It is interesting to compare Smith (288f.): 'The houses are built
of stone mostly thatched with potato stalks and these artfully kept
down by nets which cover the whole roof. These nets are made of ropes
of straw, the meshes not quite a foot square; to the ends of these stones
are tyed, which hanging down round the eves, form no disagreeable
sight.'
See also Note 2., Item iii, Chapter One, 111-113: *Roped thatch*
will hold in violent storms better than any other kind. It is found 'all
along the north-west, west and south-west coasts from Rathlin to Cape
Clear. It does not penetrate very far inland at any point.'

CHAPTER ELEVEN

1. The lake's name is spelt in a variety of ways: *Loch Errul* (O.
Survey, 1841); *Lock Iriol* (*S.Ch.,* 1940); *Loch Ioral* (*S.Ch.,* 1970);

Loch Erral—alternatively *Loch Reen* (Burke, *J.C.H.A.S.*, 14, 1908, 121); but of its meaning or origin I know nothing at all.

Smith does not give the lake a name but tells us that its water 'is of a most saponaceous abstersive quality' (Vol. 1, 288)—a delightfully eighteenth century phrase which would have cheered the hearts of Dr Johnson, or Anne Seward, or the poet James Grainger who, when writing his 'georgic' poem, 'The Sugar-Cane' in 1764 wrote to Johnson in desperation when seeking some such euphonious latinised euphemism for 'rats'.

Smith also reports that a scientist had ascertained that the water as well as 'abounding with a black kind of worm, about 2 inches long, shaped like a leech, soft and easily breaking to the touch' (*op. cit.*, 288) contained natron. The islanders call the worms *cuoga* (? *cnumhóga*= worms). See also *cu*=an insect that gnaws clothes (*An Irish-English Dictionary*, E. O'Reilly, W. Suppl. by John O'Donovan, Dublin, n.d.).

2. *Dunanore*: One of the many O'Driscoll castles along the Carbery coast, most of which were originally probably built in the thirteenth century. Of all of them this must surely be the starkest and most startling in its site and surroundings. 'When I got to the top of this castle,' wrote Smith, 'and saw the ocean roaring on all sides of the rock, I wished to be on the main land' (28f.).

The castles on Sherkin Island (Dunnalong), in Baltimore (Dunnashad), at Oldcourt, and on Cape Clear were by 1600 the last important ones controlled by the then head of the sept, Sir Fineen O'Driscoll who, according to *P.H.*, 'never in the course of his whole life had been tainted with the least spot of disloyalty' (Vol. 11, 41). See:

(i) 'The Old Castles of South-West Cork', James Coleman, *J.C.H.A.S.*, 29 (45-51); 30 (26-33); 31 (43-48);

(ii) *Donovan*, 91-92, 94-95;

(iii) 'Cape Clear Island', Jas. Burke, *J.C.H.A.S.*, 14 (2nd series), 1908, 119.

3. *The Gruagach*: The Irish word *gruagach*=enchanter, magician, here, or champion. Such a character appears in both the literary (e.g. *Toraiocht an Giolla Deacair*) and folk strands of the Fenian cycle, and so we have the 'Gruagach of the Well', the 'Gruagach of the Island', the 'Gruagach of Knowledge', and finally the 'Red-haired, one-eyed Gruagach'—a sort of Polyphemus whom Fionn blinded after he acquired the gift of knowledge from him.

See Note 9, Chapter Ten.

4. The castle held and defended by Capt. Richard Tyrell, who had fled there from commanding the vanguard at Kinsale, was captured from him by Capt. Roger Harvey.

See *Kinsale* (*The Spanish Intervention in Ireland at the end of the Elizabethan Wars*), John J. Silke, Liverpool, 1970, 154 *et passim*.

5. Kieran (Ir. *Ciarán*): *The Annals of Innisfallen*, after placing St

Kieran's birth in A.D. 352, has the following entry under the date 402: 'Ciaran and Deaglan, two bishops, came from Rome to preach the Gospel in Ireland. Ciaran having preached the Gospel in Inis-Cléire [Cape Clear] and all over Corca Laidhe [Carbery of the O'Driscoll] country founded a Bishop's see at Saighir in Ossory, and Deaglan also another Bishop's see at Ardmore in Desies' (*Miscellany*, 384).

Supporting external evidence of the existence of pre-Patrician Christian communities in Ireland comes from a contemporary writer, Prosper Tiro of Aquitaine who was living in Marseilles in the early fifth century. He tells us that in 431 Pope Celestine sent Palladins, as their first bishop, *ad Scottos in Christum credentes,* from which one is entitled to infer that there was a sufficiently large number of Christians then in the country to warrant such solicitude (see *Irish Saints in Italy*, Anselmo Tommasini, trans. by J. F. Scanlon, London and Glasgow, 1937, 38-39). The argument has also been advanced by Prof. Eoin Mac Néill, the great seminal writer on the history of early Ireland. In dealing with the claim of the *Corca Laidhe,* the inhabitants of a region roughly coterminans with the diocese of Ross, to be the first Christians in Ireland he writes: 'The claim at all events cannot be dismissed on the grounds of impossibility ... the people were always a sea-going people ... It is by no means unlikely, then, that where the Crescent could come on pirate galleys from Algiers, the Cross might well have come in some early merchant ship from Loire or Garonne' (*Phases of Irish History*, Dublin, 1919, p 162).

Indeed there seems to be no reason why contacts of various kinds with Celtic Britain, either in the way of trade or forays for plunder or to capture slaves could not have introduced some of the pagan Irish to Christianity before A.D. 400. At any rate the belief that St Ciarán of Cape Clear, St Ailbhe of Emly, St Déaglán of Ardmore, and St Ibar of Beg Erin were all pre-Patrician is a very old one, not to be lightly dismissed in a tradition of such tenacity as the Irish, despite doubts validly raised owing to difficulties in chronology, and hagiographic credulity.

St Ciarán's feast day (Ir. *féile*), March 5, has precedence over even St Patrick's Day on the island, and is a day of obligation there. The saint's cult is recalled by Trakieran (Ir. *Tráigh Chiaráin;* earlier *Fintracht Chléire*); Killkieran (Ir. *Cill Chiaráin*)—that is the church and graveyard, although the church ruins are those of a much later edifice; Tubberkieran (Ir. *Tobar Chiaráin*)—the saint's holy well; and, especially, St Ciarán's stone or 'gallawn'—a most notable relic. Other placenames, some now extinct, indicate that the saint was once venerated on the mainland of the diocese of Ross—not to mention his connection with Ossory (*Osraí*).

It is hardly necessary to add a final remark to the effect that St Ciarán of Cléire (Cape Clear) must not be confused with the later St Ciarán of Clonmacnoise. See:

(i) 'Betha Chiaráin Saighre' in *Silva Gadelica* (The Irish Text) ed. from MSS by Standish H. O'Grady, London, 1892, 1-16—reproduced by photo-lithography, Dublin, n.d. (Vol. II of *Silva Gadelica* contains the translation into English of the matter in Vol. I);

(ii) *Donovan*, 80-86;

(iii) 'Cape Clear Island', J. Burke, *J.C.H.A.S.*, 14, 1908, 115-119 (this has an exhaustive bibliography);

(iv) *Miscellany*, 20-22;

(v) *The Two Patricks,* T. F. O'Rahilly, Dublin, 1942 (pp 9, 40f.);

(vi) *Early Christian Ireland,* Máire and Liam de Paor, London, (4th impression, 1964), pp 27, 29.

6. The old church was a thatched building which, according to Smith, was 'as destitute of ornament as any barn'. Rev. Séamas Coombes, Admn., *Baile an Chaisleáin* (Castlehaven), tells me that it was replaced by the present building during the pastorate of Fr Tom Murray (1834-1840), that is to say some five to nine years after a new church had been erected in Sherkin Island (1831).

7. Not alone is there a telephone service and public water supply on the Island today but electricity is generated there. Some small industries give the much-needed employment which is needed to stem emigration.

CHAPTER TWELVE

1. With one exception (i.e. *muc mara*=sea-pig or porpoise) the original Irish does not help us very much in establishing the names of the fish in the Irish of Cape Clear, for the author simply says *madra* (a dog), *cat* (a cat), *capall* (a horse), *bó* (a cow). From the evidence I can gather the Irish equivalents as far as I can make out, are: *madra glas* (dogfish); *anglait* (cat-fish); *capall mara* (sea-horse); *bainirseach* (=*bó* or female seal). I have considerable reservations about *anglait,* although it is the Irish for 'cat-fish' in Kerry, and some also about *capall mara.* The list of fish-names, s.v. *iasc,* in 'Dornán Cnuais ó Chléire', D. Ó Floinn, *I.M.N.*, 1929, 68, is of no help in solving the problems presented in the passage.

2. 'Cape Clear is a safe garrison tonight ...': the phrase ineluctably brings to mind the well-known ninth century quatrain, of which the following is Kuno Meyer's translation:

> Bitter is the wind tonight
> It tosses the ocean's white hair:
> Tonight I fear not the fierce warriors of Norway
> Coursing on the Irish Sea.

(*Selections from Ancient Irish Poetry,* translated by Kuno Meyer, London, 1913, 101).

See also *Studies in Early Celtic Nature Poetry,* Kenneth Jackson, Cambridge, 1935, 32.

CHAPTER THIRTEEN

1. See:
  (i) 'Hearth and Chimney in the Irish House', C. Ó Danachair, *Béal.*, 16 (i-ii), 1945, 91-104;
  (ii) *Irish Heritage: The Landscape, the People, and their Work,* E. Estyn Evans, Dundalk, 1942, 73-75;
  (iii) *Joyce,* Vol. II, 142-144.

2. That remarkable Church of Ireland clergyman, scholar, and collector of Irish music, James Canon Goodman, was for a time Rector of Abbeystrewery parish near Skibbereen, during his tenure of the Professorship of Irish at Trinity College. His fame now largely arises from the results of his sedulous enthusiasm as a collector of Irish airs, and the fruits of his work in this field are preserved in four volumes (2,300 airs) in T.C.D. About 900 of the collected airs are original to him. Breandán Breathnach, in a recent article on the Kerry-born Irish-speaking Canon ('Séamas Goodman 1828-1896, Bailitheoir Ceoil', *Journal of the Kerry Archaeological and Historical Society,* No. 6, 1973, 152-171), gives the names of 240 of the airs rescued by him that happen to have titles in Irish. Although Canon Goodman confined his research to counties Kerry and Cork, it is significant to note that only five of the airs named by Ó Síocháin correspond in any way with ones in that list of 240: *An Cailín Deas Donn, An Ceannaidhe Súgach, Lá 'le Pádraig, An Maidrín Rua, Poc ar Buile.* So despite the Canon's living so close to Cape Clear much must have escaped his eager ears. The Canon is buried in the graveyard of Creagh Church beside Ilen. The meaning of the quatrain is not clear.

3. Professor Seán Ó Tuama of University College Cork thinks that the association of the wren with Druidic rites among Celtic peoples has been suggested. Perhaps the bird was used for augury and the coming of Christianity reversed the significance without altering the bird's importance. The earliest reference I have come across is in Aubrey's voluminous writings—perhaps not as odd as it may seem when we realise what an immense mine of both curious and credulous erudition he worked. Oliver Lawson Dick, the editor of *Aubrey's Brief Lives* (London, 1949), quite rightly calls Aubrey a 'man of genius'. Aubrey's story, which appears in Dick's volume, is connected with a supposed event in Letterkenny, Co. Donegal, which explains why the Irish abhor wrens (*op. cit.,* p cv). See further:
  (i) 'Some Distribution Patterns in Irish Folk Life', C. Ó Danachair, *Béal.,* 25, 1957, 120-122;
  (ii) *Timcheall Chinn Sléibhe,* Seán Ó Dálaigh, B.Á.C., 1937, 92-97;
  (iii) *Irish Heritage,* E. E. Evans, Dundalk, 1942, 157;
  (iv) *Irish Folk Ways,* E. E. Evans, London, 1972, 279.
I am aware that much more could be learned about 'hunting the wran' from the archives of the Folklore Society of Ireland.

4. *Net-making*: 'Types of nets for inshore fishing, including salmon nets, differ considerably from place to place and need study' (Estyn Evans, *Irish Heritage*, 146).

See 'Seanchas Iascaireachta is Farraige', Seán Ó hEochaidh, *Béal.*, 33, 1965, 1-96—An editorial summary in English appears on pp 87-92.

Wool and Linen: Exports of products of these were important in the Middle Ages.

Smith (1750) tells us that the island held 'a good quantity of sheep' (p 287), but a hundred and twenty-six years later when the storyteller was ten years old Daniel Donovan had this to say: 'The peculiar horned sheep, now almost extinct, and a small breed of cattle, were formerly numerous on the island' (Donovan, 112). See also:

(i) 'Focail agus Téarmaí i dtaobh Olna', Seán Ó Dubhda, *Béal.*, 16 (i-ii), 1946, 172-188;

(ii) *Joyce*, 432-433.

With regard to linen Smith says: 'But what is most pleasing, the linen manufacture has got some footing in this island, for I have seen tolerable crops of flax; most of the women spin, and it is said they purge and whiten their yarn to a degree of perfection by means of the soft water of the lake.' See Note 1, Chapter Eleven.

Unhappily, even though Cape Clear linen was still produced and sought after when the cultivation of the crop and its manufacture had ceased everywhere else in the south, it is clear from Donovan (p 110) that by 1776 this was no longer so. See:

(i) *Irish Folk Ways*, E. Estyn Evans, London and Boston, 1972, 157ff.;

(ii) *Joyce*, p 189 *et passim*.

5. The old man had personified Death, and did not relish its power of bi-location.

6. See:

(i) *Joyce*, Chapter 31;

(ii) *An Seanchaí Muimhneach*, An Seabhac, B.Á.C., 1932, 355-359;

(iii) 'Irish Wake Games', Henry Morris, *Béal.*, 8 (ii), 1938, 123-141;

(iv) *Caoineadh Airt Uí Laoghaire*, Seán Ó Tuama, B.Á.C., 1970. (Gan trácht ar an leabhar go léir is luachmhar an leabharliosta atá le fáil ar lch. 75.)

7. See:

(i) *Joyce*, 3, 439, 447;

(ii) *Irish Heritage*, E. Estyn Evans, Dundalk, 1942, pp 157, 169-171.

8. See:

(i) E. Estyn Evans, *op. cit.*, 37, 53, 121f., 146, 167; (Note that of the types of churn-dashes illustrated on p 122 the kind that was used in Galway is most like the Cape Clear model.)

(ii) *An Seanchaí Muimhneach*, An Seabhac, B.Á.C., 1932, 341-344;

(iii) *Joyce*, 137-139.

9. As Professor Pádraig Ó Fiannachta pointed out to me that this sentence reveals a delicate insight into the nature of knowledge. It would be difficult to convey the epistemological perception of the original Irish without using clumsy periphrases for, as *la verite consiste dans la nuance,* the distinction between *fios* and *eolas* lies at the very core of the original sentence's significance—and that cannot readily be carried over into English.

CHAPTER FOURTEEN

1. There is a similar adage about Leap *(An Léim),* further east in Co. Cork: *'Ní ritheann an dlí laistiar den Léim.'* Both illustrate the tenuous hold the writ of colonial law had on the south-west of Ireland, even in the hayday of the ongoing attempt to subdue the Irish nation.

2. The fight for the owernship of the land, which has been described as 'the greatest mass movement of modern Ireland', owed its beginnings to Michael Davitt (1836-1906) and Charles Stuart Parnell (1846-1891). Its great impeius dates from 1879-1882, and Davitt's own book, *The Fall of Feudalism in Ireland,* is indispensable reading for anyone wishing to understand both the man and the movement he and Parnell inspired.

CHAPTER FIFTEEN

1. Born in Skibbereen, Co. Cork, Timothy Sheehy (1855-1938) led a full and useful life in the public sphere. He became a member of the Cork County Council in 1902 and, eventually, a T.D. and 'Father of the Dáil' in 1927.

Previous to the building of North Harbour at Trakieran (ca. 1900-1903) there is evidence of interest in such a scheme going back to the early nineteenth century, as the following shows: 'Manuscript map: Cape Clear: Plan and estimate for a new quay in Clear Island. One sheet, coloured, early nineteenth century—15B. 13(3)' (see *M.S.H.I.C.,* Hayes, Vol. 7, Places A-K, Boston, 1965, p 232, G.). Nothing was done until about 1840 when a pier enclosing an inner basin was built but, as Donovan (p 66) informs us, 'as the water is very shallow in this little basin, only three or four feet at low tide, the hookers and pilot boats cannot be moored there with any safety.' Consequently, even in 1876 the boats had either to be hauled high up on the beach, or sunk, or laid up in safe mainland harbours during the winter months. This miserable plight persisted for another quarter of a century, although since the seventies the generosity of that notable philanthropist, Baroness Burdett-Coutts of the famous banking family had helped considerably in the expansion of the Cape Clear fishing fleet, and even the landlord, Sir Henry W. Becher, as Donovan (p 67) tells us, had 'kindly volunteered to pay the local contribution himself'.

2. *Sea-turn*: The eighteenth century pronunciation is preserved in the Hiberno-English use of the word in Sherkin Island, even to this day—i.e. 'say-turn'. The old term has, however, been largely replaced by the phrase 'the wind is backing' (a good sign of the weather).

In Ó Duinnín's *Foclóir* the word *saothrún* (Cape Clear dialect: *saetairn*) is glossed: 'the sun's course; *tá imeacht an tsaothrúin ar an ngaoith ó mhaidin,* the wind follows the course of the sun all day (returning to an easterly direction after sunset).' The locale he mentions is north Kerry. From information supplied by Prof. Ó Fiannachta the word is also used in west Kerry: *'saetrún, sórt dorchú ar an spéir agus deallramh doininne ná tagann i gcrích',* a definition which indicates a considerable semantic change when compared with the meaning the word has on Cape Clear.

See *O.E.D.* s.v. *sea*[23] (Special combinations).

CHAPTER SIXTEEN

1. The enormous increase in the catches made after the First World War began continued, until 1925 or thereabouts, when an American embargo put a stop to a highly profitable post-war export trade. Apart from the period of the Second Great War the subsequent decline in fishing lasted until recent years when the work of *Bord Iascaigh Mhara* (The Irish Fishery Board) brought about some improvement in the prospects of a population that had suffered dreadfully from the inroads of the Great Famine of 1846, another famine in 1862, and the consequent hemorrhage of emigration that reduced the number of people from the pre-Famine figure of almost 1,100 to something less than 200.

CHAPTER SEVENTEEN

1. This chapter heading is in perfect keeping with the occupation that is never far from the storyteller's mind—that is fishing. Equally it is just such a homely metaphor for the placid acceptance of the close of life's span as is so marked a characteristic of the Irish imagination at its best.

If we need further evidence of the part the sea has played and still plays in the life of the island we have Rev. D. Ó Floinn's two collections of Cape Clear folklore in *Béal.*: (i) 5 (ii), 1936, 111-138, a fine collection in which most of the stories have links with the sea; and (ii) 11 (i-ii), 1941, 3-77, an even more varied and revealing melânge of material of which a goodly number of items evoke the sea.

2. Manx, Irish, and Gaelic make up the c-Celtic, and Cornish, Welsh and Breton the p-Celtic group of the Celtic brànch of the Indo-

European family of languages. The parting of the ways for the two groups occurred so long ago that they are now as mutually incomprehensible as if they belonged to entirely different branches.

Both Manx and Cornish are dead tongues, the former since the late fifties of this century, the latter since ca. 1800. Efforts are being made to revive both.

As to the other four Celtic tongues one can say that despite the diverse obstacles and the crisis of the will that impede their burgeoning as full national tongues, there is no need to fear that this important Celtic branch of the great Indo-European family will die. Only 5 per cent of the 4,000 odd languages spoken in the world have attained a written form, and these four Celtic tongues are among that small percentage. As many of the remaining 95 per cent will certainly achieve a written status, it would not merely be a shame, but a major tragedy if the Celtic tongues were to fall silent just as languages of infinitely less historic importance became written vehicles of the emergent nations of the Third World.

3. This is a reference to the establishment of centres on the mainland to which families from Irish-speaking islands, or even mainland Gaeltachts, could move if they so chose. The reluctance to pull up such deep roots as Irish-speaking communities inevitably possess meant that only one such centre was finally required, that is Ráth Chairn in Co. Meath. Established in the thirties it has managed to survive, and clings tenaciously to its transplanted heritage in spite of its close proximity to a cosmopolitan capital.

4. The last note repeats the lesson of the first in Chapter One, and our narrator ends as he began—with a revealing affirmation of his awareness that perdurable bonds bind Cape Clear and many generations together in a way quite unknown to the men of the Blaskets.

SELECT BIBLIOGRAPHY

Books or articles containing matter devoted in whole or significant part to Cape Clear, its people, history, etc.

Burke, James M., 'Cape Clear Island', *J.C.H.A.S.*, 14, 1908, 115-122.

Conlon, J. P., 'Cape Clear Island', *J.C.H.A.S.*, 24, 1918, 53-61.

Cullinane, J. P., 'List of Marine Algae new to Cape Clear Island', *Cape Clear Bird Observatory Report*, No. 10, 1969, 33-35.

Donovan, Daniel, *Sketches in Carbery, County Cork*, Dublin, 1876 (Cork, 1973).

Holland, Fr W., *History of West Cork and the Diocese of Ross*, Skibbereen, 1949.

MacManus, Francis, 'Viking-Faced Cape Clear', *The Bell*, 16 (2), 1950, 24-29.

O'Donovan, John (ed.), *Miscellany of the Celtic Society*, Dublin, 1849.

Ó Floinn, D., An t-Ath., 'Dornán Cnuais ó Chuantaibh Chléire, *I.M.N.*, 1929, 62-73.

—— 'Béaloideas ó Chléire', *Béal.*, 5, 1936, 111-138.

—— 'Béaloideas ó Chléire II', *Béal.*, 11, 1941, 3-77.

—— 'Iarnís ó Chléire', *Béal.*, 12, 1942, 193-196.

O'Kelly, Michael J., 'An Example of Passage-Grave Art from County Cork', *J.C.H.A.S.*, 54, 1949, 8-10.

O'Mahony, Jeremiah, *West Cork: Parish Histories and Place-Names*, Tralee, n.d.

—— *West Cork and its Story*, Tralee, 1960.

Ó Síocháin, Conchúr, *Seanchas Chléire*, Baile Átha Cliath, 1940, 1943, 1970.

Parke, M., 'A List of the Marine Algae of Cape Clear Island', *Cape Clear Bird Observatory Report*, 1969, No. 9, 57-60.

Pococke, 'Pococke's Tour of South and South-West Ireland in 1758 (Contd.) : Notes', Pádraig Ó Maidín, *J.C.H.A.S.*, 65 (ii), 1960, 130-141.

Sharrock, J. T. R. (ed.), *The Natural History of Cape Clear Island: Oileán Cléire*, Berkhamstead, 1973.

Smith, Charles, *The Antient and Present State of the County and City of Cork,* 2 vols., Dublin, 1750 (etc.), Reprinted in 2 vols., Cork, 1973.

Somerville-Large, Peter, *The Coast of West Cork,* London, 1972.

Webster, Rev. Chancellor, 'The Diocese of Ross', *J.C.H.A.S.,* 29, 1924, 34-35.

Westropp, T. J., 'Fortified Headlands and Castles in Western County Cork' (Part 1: From Cape Clear to Dunmanus Bay), *P.R.I.A.,* Vol. XXXII, Sec. C, 249-286, 1915.

NOTE : As the *Journal of the Cork Historical and Archaeological Society* contains so many invaluable, if sometimes unreliable contributions on Cape Clear the reader interested in adding to his knowledge of the Island will find it helpful to note that two Indices have been published so far:

Index to J.C.H.A.S. (1892-1940), Cork, 1943;
Index to J.C.H.A.S. (1941-1960), Cork, 1964.

More Mercier Books

LETTERS FROM THE GREAT BLASKET
Eibhlís Ní Shúillea...

A fascinating story of a ... way of life emerges in ... which ... nd, its people

THE TAIL...
Eric Cross

'This is a darling book. The general reader will ... r delight. The folklorist already has pronounced it a treasure.'